This book is on loan from
Library Services for Schools
**www.cumbria.gov.uk/
libraries/schoolslibserv**

County Council

Printed and bound in Dubai
Author: David Ballheimer
Editor: Suhel Ahmed
Designer: Rockjaw Creative
Design Manager: Matt Drew
Picture research: Paul Langan
Production: Arlene Alexander

All facts and stats correct as of April 2021

2022 FOOTBALL LEGENDS

STATS • PROFILES • TOP PLAYERS

MORTIMER

CONTENTS

HOW TO USE THIS BOOK

Welcome to *Football Legends* — the exciting book packed with the performance stats of the biggest stars in world of football today! We have chosen more than 100 players and managers from the world's top five leagues: the Bundesliga in Germany, La Liga in Spain, France's Ligue 1, the Italian Serie A and the English Premier League.

You can use this book to figure out who you think the best performers are or you could even get together with friends and play a sort of trading-cards game, comparing the performance records of today's finest defenders, midfielders, forwards, goalkeepers and managers.

The types of stats featured for each position vary, as each position performs a specific role on the pitch. For example, a defender's main job is to stop the opposition from scoring, so the stats focus mainly on this part of their game. Likewise, a striker's tackling is not as relevant as their goal or assists tally. What you will find for all the players is the heat map, which shows how much of the pitch a player covers or, with goalkeepers, whether their strengths lie in the six-yard box or playing as sweeper-keepers who are comfortable all around the penalty area.

The stats span a player's career to date, playing for teams belonging to one of the top five European leagues. The figures have been collected from domestic league and European match appearances only, and exclude data from domestic cup, super cups or international games. This narrow data pool means that the information is instantly comparable so you can decide for yourself who truly deserves to be known as a living legend of the beautiful game.

DEFENDERS

There are different types of defenders. They cover a range of positions and have different skills. The centre-backs are the big defenders in the middle who mark the opposition strikers. Full-backs operate out wide: they are quick, agile and try to stop wide attackers from crossing balls into the box. Wing-backs play out wide, too, in front of the centre-backs, but also make attacking runs when they have the chance. Finally, the sweeper is the spare defender who is positioned behind the centre-half, ready to help the back four deal with any danger.

WHAT DO THESE STATS MEAN?

75%

AERIAL DUELS WON
This is the percentage of headers a defender has won in his own penalty area, to interrupt an opposition attack.

INTERCEPTIONS
This is the number of times a defender has successfully stopped an attack without needing to make a tackle.

BLOCKS
A shot that is intercepted by a defender – preventing his keeper from having to make a save – counts as a block.

KEY PASSES/PASS COMPLETION
A key pass is one that results in an attacking opportunity. Pass completion indicates as a percentage the player's passing accuracy.

CLEARANCES
An attack successfully foiled, either by kicking or heading the ball away from danger, is regarded as a clearance.

TACKLES
This is the number of times a defender has challenged and dispossessed the opposition without committing a foul.

JÉRÔME BOATENG

Bayern star defender Jérôme Boateng has proved himself to be one of the best in the business. He is a strong tackler, superb in the air and reads defensive situations excellently, making him a challenge for even the best centre-forwards.

NATIONALITY
German

CURRENT CLUB
Bayern Munich

BIRTHDATE	03/09/1988
POSITION	CENTRAL
HEIGHT	1.92 M
WEIGHT	90 KG
PREFERRED FOOT	RIGHT

APPEARANCES
438

BLOCKS
157

INTERCEPTIONS
748

AERIAL DUELS WON
66%

PENALTIES SCORED
0

PASS COMPLETION
85%

GOALS
10

KEY PASSES
200

CLEARANCES
1261

TACKLES
744

MAJOR CLUB HONOURS
- Bundesliga: (x 8) 2013-2020
- UEFA Champions League: 2013, 2020
- FIFA Club World Cup: 2013, 2021
- UEFA Super Cup: 2013, 2020

INTERNATIONAL HONOURS
- FIFA World Cup: 2014

ACTIVITY AREAS

NATIONALITY
Italian

CURRENT CLUB
Juventus

LEONARDO BONUCCI

Italy's vice captain Leonardo Bonucci is a strong and experienced centre-back with exceptional ball skills. He is superb at breaking up play and launching attacks with long passes. What's more, he poses a goal threat from set pieces.

BIRTHDATE	01/05/1987
POSITION	CENTRAL
HEIGHT	1.90 M
WEIGHT	85 KG
PREFERRED FOOT	RIGHT

APPEARANCES
477

BLOCKS
296

INTERCEPTIONS
826

AERIAL DUELS WON
54%

PENALTIES SCORED
0

PASS COMPLETION
87%

GOALS
27

KEY PASSES
140

CLEARANCES
2014

TACKLES
579

MAJOR CLUB HONOURS
⚽ Serie A: 2006 (Inter Milan), 2012, 2013, 2014, 2015, 2016, 2017, 2019, 2020
⚽ Coppa Italia: 2015, 2016, 2017

INTERNATIONAL HONOURS
⚽ UEFA European Championship: runner-up 2012
⚽ FIFA Confederations Cup: third place 2013

ACTIVITY AREAS

DEDRYCK BOYATA

Dedryck Boyata is equally comfortable playing at right-back or centre-half. He reads the game brilliantly and makes timely blocks and interceptions using his great positional sense before quickly distributing the ball downfield.

NATIONALITY
Belgian

CURRENT CLUB
Hertha Berlin

BIRTHDATE	28/11/1990
POSITION	CENTRAL
HEIGHT	1.88 M
WEIGHT	84 KG
PREFERRED FOOT	RIGHT

APPEARANCES
94

BLOCKS
76

INTERCEPTIONS
172

AERIAL DUELS WON
65%

PENALTIES SCORED
0

PASS COMPLETION
88%

GOALS
5

KEY PASSES
23

CLEARANCES
382

TACKLES
121

MAJOR CLUB HONOURS
⚽ FA Cup: 2011 (Manchester City)
⚽ Scottish Premiership: 2016, 2017, 2018, 2019 (Celtic)
⚽ Scottish Cup: 2017, 2018 (Celtic)

INTERNATIONAL HONOURS
⚽ FIFA World Cup: third place 2018

ACTIVITY AREAS

NATIONALITY
Italian

CURRENT CLUB
Juventus

GEORGIO CHIELLINI

The Italian is a hard-tackling centre-back whose no-nonsense approach to winning the ball makes him tough to beat. He can also play as an emergency attacker and is famous for beating his chest in celebration whenever he scores.

BIRTHDATE	14/08/1984
POSITION	CENTRAL
HEIGHT	1.87 M
WEIGHT	85 KG
PREFERRED FOOT	LEFT

BLOCKS
259

APPEARANCES
489

INTERCEPTIONS
1454

AERIAL DUELS WON
67%

PASS COMPLETION
85%

PENALTIES SCORED
0

GOALS
31

KEY PASSES
232

CLEARANCES
3127

TACKLES
1284

MAJOR CLUB HONOURS
- Serie A: 2012, 2013, 2014, 2015, 2016, 2017, 2019, 2020
- Coppa Italia: 2015, 2016, 2017, 2018

INTERNATIONAL HONOURS
- Olympic Games: bronze medal 2004
- UEFA European Championship: 2012
- FIFA Confederations Cup: third place 2013

ACTIVITY AREAS

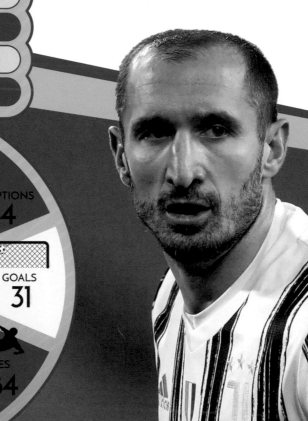

VIRGIL VAN DIJK

Dutch captain Virgil van Dijk's pace, power, passing and aerial ability have made him into one of the finest centre-backs in the world. He is also blessed with a sweet right foot and is a lethal free-kick specialist.

NATIONALITY
Dutch

CURRENT CLUB
Liverpool

BIRTHDATE	08/07/1991
POSITION	CENTRAL
HEIGHT	1.93 M
WEIGHT	92 KG
PREFERRED FOOT	RIGHT

APPEARANCES
208

INTERCEPTIONS
370

BLOCKS
107

AERIAL DUELS WON
73%

PASS COMPLETION
87%

PENALTIES SCORED
0

GOALS
18

KEY PASSES
53

CLEARANCES
1189

TACKLES
229

MAJOR CLUB HONOURS
⚽ Premier League: 2020
⚽ UEFA Champions League: 2019
⚽ FIFA Club World Cup: 2019
⚽ UEFA Super Cup: 2019

INTERNATIONAL HONOURS
⚽ UEFA Nations League: runner-up 2019

ACTIVITY AREAS

NATIONALITY
Uruguayan

CURRENT CLUB
Atlético Madrid

JOSÉ GIMÉNEZ

The Uruguayan is a tough-tackling centre-back who is quick off the mark and difficult to knock off the ball. He made his international debut when he was just 19 and has also thrived at club level since joining Atlético Madrid in 2013.

BIRTHDATE	20/01/1995
POSITION	CENTRAL
HEIGHT	1.85 M
WEIGHT	80 KG
PREFERRED FOOT	RIGHT

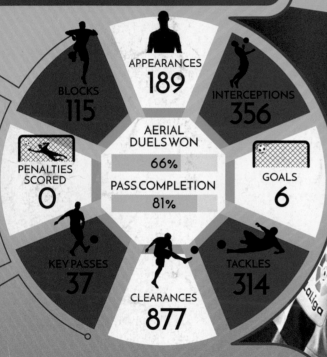

BLOCKS
115

APPEARANCES
189

INTERCEPTIONS
356

AERIAL DUELS WON
66%

PASS COMPLETION
81%

PENALTIES SCORED
0

GOALS
6

KEY PASSES
37

CLEARANCES
877

TACKLES
314

MAJOR CLUB HONOURS
- ⚽ UEFA Europa League: 2018
- ⚽ UEFA Super Cup: 2018
- ⚽ UEFA Champions League: runner-up 2014, 2016

INTERNATIONAL HONOURS
- ⚽ FIFA U-20 World Cup: runner-up 2013
- ⚽ China Cup: 2018, 2019

ACTIVITY AREAS

DIEGO GODÍN

Diego Godín is a top-class centre-half who has been one of the most rock-solid defenders in Europe over the past decade. He uses his superb positional sense to make crucial tackles and often marks the best attackers.

NATIONALITY
Uruguayan

CURRENT CLUB
Cagliari

BIRTHDATE	16/02/1986
POSITION	CENTRAL
HEIGHT	1.87 M
WEIGHT	78 KG
PREFERRED FOOT	RIGHT

BLOCKS **248**

APPEARANCES **517**

INTERCEPTIONS **1292**

PENALTIES SCORED **0**

AERIAL DUELS WON **67%**

PASS COMPLETION **79%**

GOALS **30**

KEY PASSES **107**

CLEARANCES **3146**

TACKLES **1098**

MAJOR CLUB HONOURS
⚽ La Liga: 2014 (Atlético Madrid) ⚽ UEFA Europa League: 2012, 2018 (Atlético Madrid), runner-up 2020 (Inter Milan) ⚽ UEFA Super Cup: 2010, 2012, 2018 (Atlético Madrid)

INTERNATIONAL HONOURS
⚽ Copa América: 2011
⚽ China Cup: 2018, 2019

ACTIVITY AREAS

17

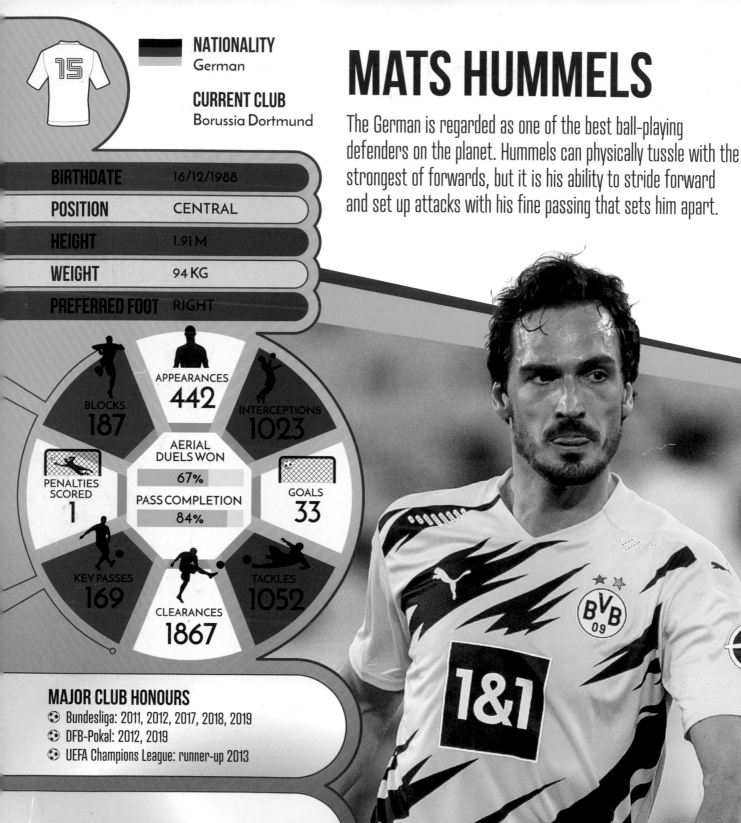

NATIONALITY
German

CURRENT CLUB
Borussia Dortmund

MATS HUMMELS

The German is regarded as one of the best ball-playing defenders on the planet. Hummels can physically tussle with the strongest of forwards, but it is his ability to stride forward and set up attacks with his fine passing that sets him apart.

BIRTHDATE	16/12/1988
POSITION	CENTRAL
HEIGHT	1.91 M
WEIGHT	94 KG
PREFERRED FOOT	RIGHT

BLOCKS
187

APPEARANCES
442

INTERCEPTIONS
1023

PENALTIES SCORED
1

AERIAL DUELS WON
67%

PASS COMPLETION
84%

GOALS
33

KEY PASSES
169

CLEARANCES
1867

TACKLES
1052

MAJOR CLUB HONOURS
- Bundesliga: 2011, 2012, 2017, 2018, 2019
- DFB-Pokal: 2012, 2019
- UEFA Champions League: runner-up 2013

INTERNATIONAL HONOURS
- FIFA World Cup: 2014

ACTIVITY AREAS

KALIDOU KOULIBALY

Kalidou Koulibaly is an aggressive centre-back, perfect for his side's high-pressing game. Extremely fast, he is capable of sprinting back to cover even if the opposition play the ball over the top or in behind his team's high defensive line.

NATIONALITY
Senegalese

CURRENT CLUB
Napoli

26

BIRTHDATE	20/06/1991
POSITION	CENTRAL
HEIGHT	1.87 M
WEIGHT	89 KG
PREFERRED FOOT	RIGHT

APPEARANCES
271

BLOCKS
218

INTERCEPTIONS
480

AERIAL DUELS WON
56%

PASS COMPLETION
88%

PENALTIES SCORED
0

GOALS
10

KEY PASSES
72

TACKLES
543

CLEARANCES
989

MAJOR CLUB HONOURS
- ⚽ Belgian Cup: 2013 (Genk)
- ⚽ Coppa Italia: 2020

INTERNATIONAL HONOURS
- ⚽ None to date

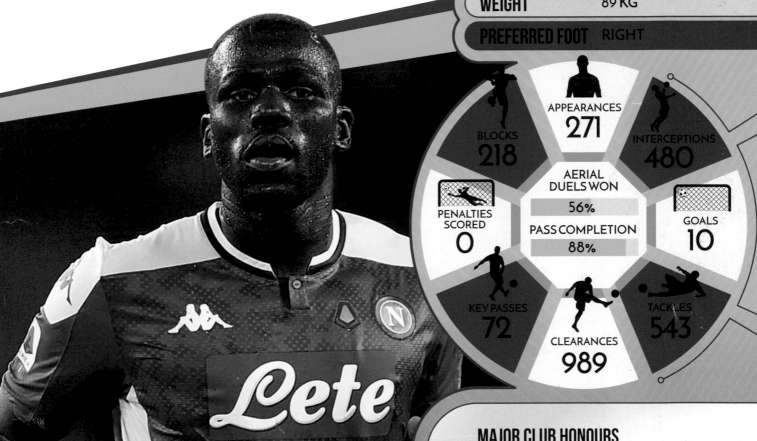

ACTIVITY AREAS

14

NATIONALITY
French

CURRENT CLUB
Manchester City

AYMERIC LAPORTE

Aymeric Laporte has become one of Europe's best central defenders. Very strong, he is powerful in the tackle, excellent in the air and a good organiser at the back. Laporte can also start attacks with his precise passing out of defence.

BIRTHDATE	27/05/1994
POSITION	CENTRAL
HEIGHT	1.91 M
WEIGHT	86 KG
PREFERRED FOOT	LEFT

BLOCKS
119

APPEARANCES
283

INTERCEPTIONS
595

AERIAL DUELS WON
65%

PASS COMPLETION
86%

PENALTIES SCORED
0

GOALS
13

KEY PASSES
68

CLEARANCES
1096

TACKLES
500

MAJOR CLUB HONOURS
⚽ Premier League: 2018, 2019
⚽ FA Cup: 2019

INTERNATIONAL HONOURS
⚽ UEFA European U-19 Championship: runner-up 2013

ACTIVITY AREAS

20

HARRY MAGUIRE

Harry Maguire attended a EURO 2016 match as a fan and only two years later played for England at the 2018 World Cup. He is a technically gifted centre-back, superb in the air, a strong tackler and very capable with the ball at his feet.

 **NATIONALITY**
English

CURRENT CLUB
Manchester United

BIRTHDATE	05/03/1993
POSITION	CENTRAL
HEIGHT	1.94 M
WEIGHT	100 KG
PREFERRED FOOT	RIGHT

APPEARANCES
187

BLOCKS
129

INTERCEPTIONS
309

PENALTIES SCORED
0

AERIAL DUELS WON
72%

PASS COMPLETION
84%

GOALS
10

KEY PASSES
65

CLEARANCES
807

TACKLES
228

MAJOR CLUB HONOURS
⚽ Football League Championship: play-offs 2016 (Hull City)

INTERNATIONAL HONOURS
⚽ UEFA Nations League: third place 2019

ACTIVITY AREAS

21

5

NATIONALITY
Brazilian

CURRENT CLUB
Paris Saint-Germain

MARQUINHOS

Marquinhos is a clever defender. He may not be a powerhouse like many of today's top-class centre-backs, but has the speed, agility and intelligence to mark the quickest forwards, plus he can be very effective going forward.

BIRTHDATE	14/05/1994
POSITION	CENTRAL
HEIGHT	1.83 M
WEIGHT	75 KG
PREFERRED FOOT	RIGHT

APPEARANCES
289

BLOCKS
173

INTERCEPTIONS
449

AERIAL DUELS WON
59%

PASS COMPLETION
92%

PENALTIES SCORED
0

GOALS
23

KEY PASSES
56

TACKLES
480

CLEARANCES
1047

MAJOR CLUB HONOURS
⚽ Ligue 1: 2014, 2015, 2016, 2018, 2019, 2020
⚽ UEFA Champions League: runner-up 2020
⚽ Coupe de France: 2015, 2016, 2017, 2018, 2020

INTERNATIONAL HONOURS
⚽ Copa América: 2019
⚽ Olympic Games: 2018

ACTIVITY AREAS

YUTO NAGATOMO

The experienced Yuto Nagatomo is a much-travelled full-back who has played throughout Europe. He has excellent tackling technique, is surprisingly good at winning defensive headers and is great at stopping not only wingers' dangerous runs, but their crosses too.

NATIONALITY
Japanese

CURRENT CLUB
Marseille

BIRTHDATE	12/09/1986
POSITION	FULL BACK
HEIGHT	1.70 M
WEIGHT	68 KG
PREFERRED FOOT	BOTH

APPEARANCES
242

BLOCKS
33

INTERCEPTIONS
364

AERIAL DUELS WON
40%

PASS COMPLETION
82%

PENALTIES SCORED
0

GOALS
10

KEY PASSES
154

CLEARANCES
567

TACKLES
424

MAJOR CLUB HONOURS
⚽ J-League Cup: 2009 (FC Tokyo)
⚽ Coppa Italia: 2011 (Inter Milan)
⚽ Turkish Super League: 2018, 2019 (Galatasaray)
⚽ Turkish Cup: 2019 (Galatasaray)

INTERNATIONAL HONOURS
⚽ AFC Asian Cup: 2011, runner-up 2019

ACTIVITY AREAS

23

NATIONALITY
French

CURRENT CLUB
Bayern Munich

BENJAMIN PAVARD

One of the stars to emerge at the 2018 World Cup, Benjamin Pavard has since matured into a technically brilliant defender at Bayern Munich. He is usually in the right place at the right time to tackle or intercept dangerous passes.

BIRTHDATE	28/03/1996.
POSITION	CENTRAL
HEIGHT	1.86 M
WEIGHT	76 KG
PREFERRED FOOT	RIGHT

BLOCKS
71

APPEARANCES
134

INTERCEPTIONS
257

PENALTIES SCORED
0

AERIAL DUELS WON
58%

PASS COMPLETION
86%

GOALS
5

KEY PASSES
53

CLEARANCES
488

TACKLES
170

MAJOR CLUB HONOURS
- ⚽ Bundesliga: 2020
- ⚽ UEFA Champions League: 2020
- ⚽ UEFA Super Cup: 2020
- ⚽ FIFA Club World Cup: 2021

INTERNATIONAL HONOURS
- ⚽ FIFA World Cup: 2018

ACTIVITY AREAS

GERARD PIQUÉ

Gerard Piqué is still classed among the best defenders in the world. Normally a centre-half, he can also play at sweeper or in front of the defence. He is an accurate passer, plus his height gives him an aerial advantage over his opponents.

NATIONALITY
Spanish

CURRENT CLUB
Barcelona

BIRTHDATE	02/02/1987
POSITION	CENTRAL
HEIGHT	1.94 M
WEIGHT	85 KG
PREFERRED FOOT	RIGHT

APPEARANCES
510

BLOCKS
262

INTERCEPTIONS
743

AERIAL DUELS WON
66%

PENALTIES SCORED
0

PASS COMPLETION
90%

GOALS
45

KEY PASSES
86

CLEARANCES
2233

TACKLES
800

MAJOR CLUB HONOURS
⚽ La Liga: 2009, 2010, 2011, 2013, 2015, 2016, 2018, 2019 ⚽ UEFA Champions League: 2008, 2009, 2011, 2015 ⚽ UEFA Super Cup: 2009, 2015 ⚽ FIFA Club World Cup: 2009, 2011, 2015

INTERNATIONAL HONOURS
⚽ FIFA World Cup: 2010
⚽ UEFA European Championship: 2012

ACTIVITY AREAS

25

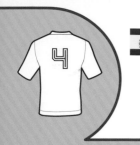

4

NATIONALITY
Spanish

CURRENT CLUB
Real Madrid

SERGIO RAMOS

Centre-back Sergio Ramos has been a star at Real Madrid ever since he joined the club in 2005. Not only is he a skilled defender and great team leader, but is also known for regularly scoring important goals for his team.

BIRTHDATE	30/03/1986
POSITION	CENTRAL
HEIGHT	1.84 M
WEIGHT	82 KG
PREFERRED FOOT	RIGHT

APPEARANCES
642

BLOCKS
298

INTERCEPTIONS
1429

AERIAL DUELS WON
67%

PASS COMPLETION
87%

PENALTIES SCORED
18

GOALS
90

KEY PASSES
283

CLEARANCES
2661

TACKLES
1317

MAJOR CLUB HONOURS
- ⚽ La Liga: 2007, 2008, 2012, 2017, 2020
- ⚽ UEFA Champions League: 2014, 2016, 2017, 2018
- ⚽ UEFA Super Cup: 2014, 2016, 2017
- ⚽ FIFA Club World Cup: 2014, 2016, 2017

INTERNATIONAL HONOURS
- ⚽ FIFA World Cup: 2010
- ⚽ UEFA European Championship: 2008, 2012
- ⚽ FIFA Confederations Cup: third place 2009, runner-up 2013

ACTIVITY AREAS

HIROKI SAKAI

Hiroki Sakai is one of the few Japanese defenders to play top-level European club football. Normally a right-back, Sakai can also adapt his game to play in other positions. He is an expert ball-winner who is fast and always alert to danger.

NATIONALITY
Japanese

CURRENT CLUB
Marseille

BIRTHDATE	12/04/1990
POSITION	FULL-BACK
HEIGHT	1.83 M
WEIGHT	70 KG
PREFERRED FOOT	RIGHT

APPEARANCES
256

BLOCKS
76

INTERCEPTIONS
454

AERIAL DUELS WON
61%

PENALTIES SCORED
0

PASS COMPLETION
79%

GOALS
4

KEY PASSES
154

CLEARANCES
694

TACKLES
579

MAJOR CLUB HONOURS
⚽ UEFA Europa League: runner-up 2018

INTERNATIONAL HONOURS
⚽ AFC Asian Cup: runner-up 2019

ACTIVITY AREAS

 NATIONALITY
Brazilian

CURRENT CLUB
Chelsea

THIAGO SILVA

Players past and present rate Thiago Silva as one of the best-ever central defenders to play the game. In addition to his technical strengths, he is a natural leader who is able to inspire team-mates to raise their game in the heat of battle.

BIRTHDATE	22/09/1984
POSITION	CENTRAL
HEIGHT	1.83 M
WEIGHT	79 KG
PREFERRED FOOT	RIGHT

APPEARANCES
399

BLOCKS
268

INTERCEPTIONS
909

AERIAL DUELS WON
72%

PASS COMPLETION
93%

PENALTIES SCORED
0

GOALS
20

KEY PASSES
88

TACKLES
621

CLEARANCES
2161

MAJOR CLUB HONOURS
- ⚽ Serie A: 2011 (Inter Milan)
- ⚽ Ligue 1: (x 7) 2013–2020 (PSG)
- ⚽ Coupe de France: 2015, 2016, 2017, 2018, 2020 (PSG)

INTERNATIONAL HONOURS
- ⚽ FIFA Confederations Cup; 2013
- ⚽ Copa América: 2019

ACTIVITY AREAS

MILAN ŠKRINIAR

Centre-back Milan Škriniar is a forceful tackler, strong in the air and combative on the ground. But what sets Škriniar apart are his ball-playing skills and ability to stay calm under pressure and pick out intelligent passes.

NATIONALITY
Slovakian

CURRENT CLUB
Inter Milan

BIRTHDATE	11/02/1995
POSITION	CENTRAL
HEIGHT	1.87 M
WEIGHT	80 KG
PREFERRED FOOT	LEFT

APPEARANCES
187

INTERCEPTIONS
193

BLOCKS
117

AERIAL DUELS WON
52%

PASS COMPLETION
92%

PENALTIES SCORED
0

GOALS
7

KEY PASSES
39

TACKLES
318

CLEARANCES
690

MAJOR CLUB HONOURS
- ⚽ UEFA Europa League: runner-up 2020
- ⚽ Slovak Super Liga: 2012 (MŠK Žilina)
- ⚽ Slovak Cup: 2012 (MŠK Žilina)

INTERNATIONAL HONOURS
- ⚽ King's Cup: 2018

ACTIVITY AREAS

5

NATIONALITY
French

CURRENT CLUB
RB Leipzig

DAYOT UPAMECANO

This rising star has blistering pace which helps him to make important tackles, interceptions and win headers. But Upamecano's standout talent is his ability with the ball at his feet — a quality that complements his passing accuracy.

BIRTHDATE	27/10/1998
POSITION	CENTRAL
HEIGHT	1.86 M
WEIGHT	90 KG
PREFERRED FOOT	RIGHT

BLOCKS
59

APPEARANCES
140

INTERCEPTIONS
247

AERIAL DUELS WON
63%

PASS COMPLETION
86%

PENALTIES SCORED
0

GOALS
4

KEY PASSES
33

CLEARANCES
499

TACKLES
285

MAJOR CLUB HONOURS
⚽ None to date

INTERNATIONAL HONOURS
⚽ UEFA European U-17 Championship: 2015

ACTIVITY AREAS

RAPHAËL VARANE

While most defenders shine in their late 20s, Raphaël Varane was already a star in his teens. Accurate with either foot, an excellent tackler and great in the air, Varane can also launch attacks with his sharp passing and even score goals.

NATIONALITY
French

CURRENT CLUB
Real Madrid

BIRTHDATE	25/04/1993
POSITION	CENTRAL
HEIGHT	1.91 M
WEIGHT	81 KG
PREFERRED FOOT	RIGHT

APPEARANCES
337

BLOCKS
166

INTERCEPTIONS
506

AERIAL DUELS WON
69%

PENALTIES SCORED
0

PASS COMPLETION
88%

GOALS
12

KEY PASSES
56

CLEARANCES
1501

TACKLES
399

MAJOR CLUB HONOURS
⚽ La Liga: 2012, 2017, 2020
⚽ UEFA Champions League: 2014, 2016, 2017, 2018
⚽ UEFA Super Cup: 2014, 2016, 2017
⚽ FIFA Club World Cup: 2014, 2016, 2017, 2018

INTERNATIONAL HONOURS
⚽ FIFA World Cup: 2018

ACTIVITY AREAS

MIDFIELDERS

Midfielders are the heartbeat of a team. Not only do they play between the forwards and the defenders but they also help out their team-mates at both ends. Midfielders fall into one of four main categories: 1) defensive midfielders, who sit in front of the back four and are great tacklers; 2) the attacking full-backs operating on the wings who whip crosses into the box; 3) the central midfielders who are brilliant at setting up and then joining attacks, as well as helping out in defence whenever needed; 4) the playmakers — these are the stars who build the attack with their creative play.

WHAT DO THE STATS MEAN?

ASSISTS
A pass, cross or header to a team-mate who then scores counts as an assist. This stat also includes a deflected shot that is converted by a team-mate.

SHOTS
Any deliberate strike on goal counts as a shot. The strike does not have to be on target or force a save from the keeper.

CHANCES CREATED
Any pass that results in a shot at goal (whether or not the goal is scored) is regarded as a chance created.

TACKLES
This is the number of times the player has challenged and dispossessed the opposition without committing a foul.

DRIBBLES
This is the number of times the player has gone past an opponent while running with the ball.

75%

SUCCESSFUL PASSES
This shows as a percentage how successful the midfielder is at finding team-mates with passes, whether over five or 60 yards.

Did you
know?

In top-level football, midfielders tend to cover the most ground during the course of a match. A midfielder playing the full 90 minutes will usually run anywhere between 9.5 and 12km.

17

NATIONALITY
Belgian

CURRENT CLUB
Manchester City

BIRTHDATE	28/06/1991
POSITION	ATTACKING
HEIGHT	1.81 M
WEIGHT	68 KG
PREFERRED FOOT	RIGHT

KEVIN DE BRUYNE

Kevin De Bruyne ranks as one of the finest attacking midfielders in the game today. Strong and technically brilliant, he can break up play at one end and almost immediately blast a 25-metre shot into the opposite goal.

APPEARANCES
321

ASSISTS
132

DRIBBLES
1032

PASSES
16006
SUCCESSFUL PASSES
80%

PENALTIES SCORED
5

GOALS
78

SHOTS
782

CHANCES CREATED
942

TACKLES
411

MAJOR CLUB HONOURS
⚽ Premier League: 2018, 2019
⚽ FA Cup: 2019

INTERNATIONAL HONOURS
⚽ FIFA World Cup: third place 2018

ACTIVITY AREAS

34

SERGIO BUSQUETS

Sergio Busquets plays as a deep midfielder who dictates the team's build-up play with clever, short and longer passes. He is great at stopping attacks before they become dangerous and then making passes to launch his team's raids.

NATIONALITY
Spanish

CURRENT CLUB
Barcelona

BIRTHDATE	16/07/1988
POSITION	DEFENSIVE
HEIGHT	1.89 M
WEIGHT	76 KG
PREFERRED FOOT	RIGHT

APPEARANCES
525

ASSISTS
34

DRIBBLES
379

PASSES
37714

SUCCESSFUL PASSES
91%

PENALTIES SCORED
0

GOALS
13

SHOTS
119

CHANCES CREATED
315

TACKLES
1365

MAJOR CLUB HONOURS
- La Liga: 2009, 2010, 2011, 2013, 2015, 2016, 2018, 2019
- UEFA Champions League: 2009, 2011, 2015
- UEFA Super Cup: 2009, 2011, 2015
- FIFA Club World Cup: 2009, 2011, 2015

INTERNATIONAL HONOURS
- FIFA World Cup: 2010
- UEFA European Championship: 2012
- FIFA Confederations Cup: runner-up 2013

ACTIVITY AREAS

27

NATIONALITY
German

CURRENT CLUB
Borussia Dortmund

EMRE CAN

Having been a defender earlier in his career, Emre Can has grown into a classy central midfielder. He combines his excellent tackling strength with his midfielder's instincts to thread passes to team-mates in attacking positions.

BIRTHDATE	12/01/1994
POSITION	CENTRAL
HEIGHT	1.86 M
WEIGHT	86 KG
PREFERRED FOOT	RIGHT

ASSISTS
16

APPEARANCES
265

DRIBBLES
513

PENALTIES SCORED
1

PASSES
13033

SUCCESSFUL PASSES
84%

GOALS
23

SHOTS
271

CHANCES CREATED
183

TACKLES
601

MAJOR CLUB HONOURS
⚽ Bundesliga: 2013 (Bayern Munich) ⚽ UEFA Champions League: 2013 (Bayern Munich), runner-up 2018 (Liverpool) ⚽ UEFA Europa League: runner-up 2016 (Liverpool) ⚽ Serie A: 2019 (Juventus)

INTERNATIONAL HONOURS
⚽ FIFA Confederations Cup: 2017

ACTIVITY AREAS

CASEMIRO

Casemiro's strengths are great energy, a high work-rate and good support play. Strong, mobile and hard-tackling, his best position is as a defensive midfielder, though his mobility helps get from box to box and he can also play at centre-back.

APPEARANCES
248

ASSISTS
17

DRIBBLES
181

PENALTIES SCORED
0

PASSES
12927

SUCCESSFUL PASSES
86%

GOALS
29

SHOTS
264

CHANCES CREATED
136

TACKLES
786

MAJOR CLUB HONOURS
- ⚽ UEFA Champions League: 2014, 2016, 2017, 2018
- ⚽ UEFA Super Cup: 2014, 2016, 2017 ⚽ FIFA Club World Cup: 2014, 2017, 2018 ⚽ La Liga: 2017, 2020
- ⚽ Copa del Rey: 2014

INTERNATIONAL HONOURS
- ⚽ FIFA U-20 World Cup: 2011
- ⚽ Copa América: 2019

ACTIVITY AREAS

NATIONALITY
Brazilian

CURRENT CLUB
Barcelona

PHILIPPE COUTINHO

Philippe Coutinho brings Brazilian flair to the pitch whenever he plays. Highly skilled with both feet, he is the type of attacking midfielder opposition defenders hate to face. Coutinho scores an average of almost one goal every four games.

BIRTHDATE	12/06/1992
POSITION	ATTACKING
HEIGHT	1.72 M
WEIGHT	68 KG
PREFERRED FOOT	RIGHT

ASSISTS
64

APPEARANCES
346

DRIBBLES
1297

PENALTIES SCORED
2

PASSES
13456
SUCCESSFUL PASSES
82%

GOALS
87

SHOTS
946

CHANCES CREATED
543

TACKLES
410

MAJOR CLUB HONOURS
⚽ La Liga: 2018, 2019
⚽ Bundesliga: 2020 (Bayern Munich)
⚽ Copa del Rey: 2018
⚽ Copa Italia: 2011 (Inter Milan)

INTERNATIONAL HONOURS
⚽ FIFA U-20 World Cup: 2011
⚽ Copa América: 2019

ACTIVITY AREAS

38

JULIAN DRAXLER

Julian Draxler is a thrill to watch! He has the pace to get past the defence and deliver a dangerous cross or pass with pinpoint accuracy. If going for goal himself, he is capable of an impressive left-footed strike.

NATIONALITY
German

CURRENT CLUB
Paris Saint-Germain

BIRTHDATE	20/09/1993
POSITION	ATTACKING
HEIGHT	1.85 M
WEIGHT	72 KG
PREFERRED FOOT	RIGHT

APPEARANCES
329

ASSISTS
47

DRIBBLES
1077

PENALTIES SCORED
0

PASSES
10716

SUCCESSFUL PASSES
86%

GOALS
47

SHOTS
434

CHANCES CREATED
425

TACKLES
318

MAJOR CLUB HONOURS
- Ligue 1: 2018, 2019, 2020
- UEFA Champions League: runner-up 2020
- Coupe de France: 2017, 2018, 2020
- DFB-Pokal: 2011 (Schalke 04)

INTERNATIONAL HONOURS
- FIFA World Cup: 2014
- FIFA Confederations Cup: 2017

ACTIVITY AREAS

24

NATIONALITY
Danish

CURRENT CLUB
Inter Milan

CHRISTIAN ERIKSEN

Christian Eriksen has a great footballing brain which allows him to be a key player as a No.10, or central midfielder. He is excellent at setting up chances for his forwards or scoring with his dangerous right foot, especially free-kicks.

BIRTHDATE	14/02/1992
POSITION	ATTACKING
HEIGHT	1.82 M
WEIGHT	76 KG
PREFERRED FOOT	BOTH

APPEARANCES
348

ASSISTS
85

DRIBBLES
573

PASSES
16538

PENALTIES SCORED
0

SUCCESSFUL PASSES
82%

GOALS
67

SHOTS
791

CHANCES CREATED
808

TACKLES
374

MAJOR CLUB HONOURS
⚽ UEFA Europa League: runner-up 2020
⚽ UEFA Champions League: runner-up 2019 (Tottenham Hotspur)
⚽ Eredivisie: 2011, 2012, 2013 (Ajax)

INTERNATIONAL HONOURS
⚽ None to date

ACTIVITY AREAS

FABINHO

After a slow start to his Liverpool career, Fabinho has now become a fan favourite. Tall and strong, he is a master at keeping possession for his team and starting the attack from deep. His heat map shows how dominant he is in midfield.

 **NATIONALITY**
Brazilian

CURRENT CLUB
Liverpool

BIRTHDATE	23/10/1993
POSITION	DEFENSIVE
HEIGHT	1.88 M
WEIGHT	78 KG
PREFERRED FOOT	RIGHT

APPEARANCES
301

ASSISTS
18

DRIBBLES
382

PASSES
15293

SUCCESSFUL PASSES
85%

PENALTIES SCORED
17

GOALS
28

SHOTS
173

CHANCES CREATED
193

TACKLES
824

MAJOR CLUB HONOURS
- ⚽ Premier League: 2020
- ⚽ UEFA Champions League: 2019
- ⚽ UEFA Super Cup: 2019
- ⚽ Ligue 1: 2017 (Monaco)

INTERNATIONAL HONOURS
- ⚽ Copa América: 2019

ACTIVITY AREAS

18

NATIONALITY
Portuguese

CURRENT CLUB
Manchester United

BRUNO FERNANDES

Bruno Fernandes shines as a central or attacking midfielder. A sound defensive player, he has a fantastic eye for creating chances with through balls, driving powerful shots from long range and is superb with penalties and free-kicks.

BIRTHDATE	08/09/1994
POSITION	ATTACKING
HEIGHT	1.79 M
WEIGHT	69 KG
PREFERRED FOOT	RIGHT

ASSISTS **42**

APPEARANCES **204**

DRIBBLES **367**

PASSES **7829**

SUCCESSFUL PASSES **76%**

PENALTIES SCORED **21**

GOALS **60**

SHOTS **484**

CHANCES CREATED **364**

TACKLES **290**

MAJOR CLUB HONOURS
⚽ Taça de Portugal: 2019 (Sporting CP)
⚽ Taça de Liga: 2018, 2019 (Sporting CP)

INTERNATIONAL HONOURS
⚽ UEFA Nations League: 2019

ACTIVITY AREAS

ROBERTO FIRMINO

Roberto Firmino is a box-to-box midfielder with great energy and a perfect passing technique over both long and short distances. He usually plays as a second attacker with a superb left foot, but also surprises defenders with his heading ability.

 **NATIONALITY**
Brazilian

CURRENT CLUB
Liverpool

BIRTHDATE	02/10/1991
POSITION	ATT/STRIKER
HEIGHT	1.81 M
WEIGHT	76 KG
PREFERRED FOOT	RIGHT

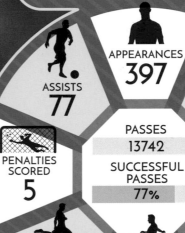

ASSISTS
77

APPEARANCES
397

DRIBBLES
1545

PENALTIES SCORED
5

PASSES
13742

SUCCESSFUL PASSES
77%

GOALS
117

SHOTS
924

CHANCES CREATED
622

TACKLES
738

MAJOR CLUB HONOURS
- Premier League: 2020
- UEFA Champions League: 2019
- UEFA Europa League: runner-up 2016
- UEFA Super Cup: 2019
- FIFA Club World Cup: 2019

INTERNATIONAL HONOURS
- Copa América: 2019

ACTIVITY AREAS

NATIONALITY
Belgian

CURRENT CLUB
Real Madrid

EDEN HAZARD

Playing as an attacking midfielder or winger, Eden Hazard is one of the best at running with the ball and taking players on. He is known for his creativity, speed and technical ability, and is capable of changing the game with a turn of pace or dribble.

BIRTHDATE	07/01/1991
POSITION	SECOND STRIKER
HEIGHT	1.75 M
WEIGHT	74 KG
PREFERRED FOOT	BOTH

APPEARANCES
501

ASSISTS
108

DRIBBLES
2690

PASSES
20685

SUCCESSFUL PASSES
83%

PENALTIES SCORED
32

GOALS
138

SHOTS
893

CHANCES CREATED
1059

TACKLES
311

MAJOR CLUB HONOURS
⚽ La Liga: 2020 ⚽ Premier League: 2015, 2017 (Chelsea)
⚽ Ligue 1: 2011 (Lille)
⚽ UEFA Europa League: 2013, 2019 (Chelsea)
⚽ FIFA Club World Cup: runner-up 2012 (Chelsea)

INTERNATIONAL HONOURS
⚽ FIFA World Cup: third-place 2018

ACTIVITY AREAS

FRENKIE DE JONG

Frenkie de Jong has been an outstanding talent ever since he burst on to the scene as a teenager. His close control, accuracy, work rate, passing accuracy and movement have seen him being compared to the great Johan Cruyff.

NATIONALITY
Dutch

CURRENT CLUB
Barcelona

BIRTHDATE	12/05/1997
POSITION	CENTRAL
HEIGHT	1.80 M
WEIGHT	74 KG
PREFERRED FOOT	RIGHT

APPEARANCES
89

ASSISTS
7

DRIBBLES
163

PENALTIES SCORED
0

PASSES
5774

SUCCESSFUL PASSES
92%

GOALS
5

SHOTS
22

CHANCES CREATED
74

TACKLES
113

MAJOR CLUB HONOURS
⚽ Eredivisie: 2019 (Ajax)
⚽ KNVB Cup: 2019 (Ajax)
⚽ UEFA Europa League: runner-up 2017 (Ajax)

INTERNATIONAL HONOURS
⚽ UEFA Nations League: runner-up: 2019

ACTIVITY AREAS

 NATIONALITY
French

CURRENT CLUB
Chelsea

N'GOLO KANTÉ

Defensive midfielder N'Golo Kanté has pace, boundless energy and great positional awareness. He frequently breaks up attacks with timely tackles, blocks and interceptions, then makes accurate passes. He has an eye for goal, too.

BIRTHDATE	29/03/1991
POSITION	CENTRAL
HEIGHT	1.68 M
WEIGHT	68 KG
PREFERRED FOOT	RIGHT

ASSISTS
18

APPEARANCES
255

DRIBBLES
507

PASSES
12902
SUCCESSFUL PASSES
86%

PENALTIES SCORED
0

GOALS
12

SHOTS
174

CHANCES CREATED
246

TACKLES
831

MAJOR CLUB HONOURS

⚽ Premier League: 2016 (Leicester City) 2017
⚽ UEFA Europa League: 2019
⚽ FA Cup: 2018

INTERNATIONAL HONOURS

⚽ FIFA World Cup: 2018
⚽ UEFA European Championship: runner-up 2016

ACTIVITY AREAS

46

SERGEJ MILINKOVIĆ-SAVIĆ

Effective in and around both penalty areas, Sergej Milinković-Savić is a top-class midfielder. He is blessed with great energy and sound technique, and is also good at stopping opposition attacks and launching his own team's raids.

NATIONALITY
Serbian

CURRENT CLUB
Lazio

BIRTHDATE	27/02/1995
POSITION	CENTRAL
HEIGHT	1.91 M
WEIGHT	76 KG
PREFERRED FOOT	RIGHT

APPEARANCES
218

ASSISTS
29

DRIBBLES
459

PASSES
9696

SUCCESSFUL PASSES
77%

PENALTIES SCORED
0

GOALS
40

SHOTS
457

CHANCES CREATED
281

TACKLES
353

MAJOR CLUB HONOURS
⚽ Coppa Italia: 2019

INTERNATIONAL HONOURS
⚽ UEFA European U-19 Championship: 2013
⚽ FIFA U-20 World Cup: 2015

ACTIVITY AREAS

10

NATIONALITY
Croatian

CURRENT CLUB
Real Madrid

LUKA MODRIĆ

Playmaker Luka Modrić is often at the heart of his team's best attacking moves. He has a great footballing brain, can deliver long and short passes with both feet and strike powerful long-range shots, especially free-kicks.

BIRTHDATE	09/09/1985
POSITION	ATTACKING
HEIGHT	1.72 M
WEIGHT	66 KG
PREFERRED FOOT	RIGHT

ASSISTS
68

APPEARANCES
491

DRIBBLES
1271

PENALTIES SCORED
3

PASSES
27366
SUCCESSFUL PASSES
89%

GOALS
41

SHOTS
614

CHANCES CREATED
777

TACKLES
702

MAJOR CLUB HONOURS
⚽ La Liga: 2017, 2020
⚽ UEFA Champions League: 2014, 2016, 2017, 2018
⚽ UEFA Super Cup: 2014, 2016, 2017
⚽ FIFA Club World Cup: 2014, 2016, 2017, 2018

INTERNATIONAL HONOURS
⚽ FIFA World Cup: runner-up 2018

ACTIVITY AREAS

JOÃO MOUTINHO

The experienced João Moutinho has been a quality attacking or defensive midfielder for many years. He has great anticipation and positional awareness, as well as being an ace at set-pieces, shooting from distance and delivering long passes to team-mates.

NATIONALITY
Portuguese

CURRENT CLUB
Wolverhampton Wanderers

28

BIRTHDATE	08/09/1986
POSITION	CENTRAL
HEIGHT	1.70 M
WEIGHT	61 KG
PREFERRED FOOT	RIGHT

APPEARANCES
383

ASSISTS
55

DRIBBLES
312

PENALTIES SCORED
1

PASSES
18827
SUCCESSFUL PASSES
85%

GOALS
18

SHOTS
330

CHANCES CREATED
638

TACKLES
792

MAJOR CLUB HONOURS
- ⚽ Ligue 1: 2017 (Monaco)
- ⚽ UEFA Europa League: runner-up 2005 (Sporting Clube)
- ⚽ Primeira Liga: 2011, 2012, 2013 (Porto)

INTERNATIONAL HONOURS
- ⚽ UEFA European Championship: 2016
- ⚽ UEFA Nations League: 2019
- ⚽ FIFA Confederations Cup: 2017

ACTIVITY AREAS

49

25

NATIONALITY
German

CURRENT CLUB
Bayern Munich

THOMAS MÜLLER

Thomas Müller is a dangerous attacking midfielder, who scores countless goals playing just behind a lone striker. The German powerhouse is mentally strong, tactically clever and great at finding holes in the opposition's defence.

BIRTHDATE	13/09/1989
POSITION	SECOND STRIKER
HEIGHT	1.86 M
WEIGHT	75 KG
PREFERRED FOOT	RIGHT

ASSISTS
150

APPEARANCES
499

DRIBBLES
959

PASSES
16144

SUCCESSFUL
PASSES
77%

PENALTIES
SCORED
22

GOALS
176

SHOTS
1015

CHANCES
CREATED
931

TACKLES
536

MAJOR CLUB HONOURS
- ⚽ Bundesliga: x 9 (between 2010 and 2020)
- ⚽ UEFA Champions League: 2013, 2020
- ⚽ UEFA Super Cup: 2013, 2020
- ⚽ FIFA Club World Cup: 2013, 2021

INTERNATIONAL HONOURS
- ⚽ FIFA World Cup: 2014, third place 2010

ACTIVITY AREAS

MIRALEM PJANIĆ

An old-fashioned playmaker, Miralem Pjanić is great on the ball and can spray passes all around the pitch. His right-foot is like a magic wand at free-kicks, curling or driving shots past the wall and he creates chances for team-mates, too.

NATIONALITY
Bosnian

CURRENT CLUB
Barcelona

BIRTHDATE	02/04/1990
POSITION	CENTRAL
HEIGHT	1.78 M
WEIGHT	72 KG
PREFERRED FOOT	BOTH

APPEARANCES
504

ASSISTS
97

DRIBBLES
744

PENALTIES SCORED
7

PASSES
25971
SUCCESSFUL PASSES
87%

GOALS
66

SHOTS
782

CHANCES CREATED
930

TACKLES
689

MAJOR CLUB HONOURS
⚽ Serie A: 2017, 2018, 2019, 2020 (Juventus)
⚽ Coppa Italia: 2017, 2018 (Juventus)

INTERNATIONAL HONOURS
⚽ None to date

ACTIVITY AREAS

6

NATIONALTIY
French

CURRENT CLUB
Manchester United

PAUL POGBA

Known for his strength, speed and athleticism, Paul Pogba glides across the pitch on and off the ball, stopping attacks at one end before finishing off his team's rapid counter-attack. Good with both feet, Pogba is lethal in front of goal.

BIRTHDATE	15/03/1993
POSITION	CENTRAL
HEIGHT	1.91 M
WEIGHT	84 KG
PREFERRED FOOT	RIGHT

APPEARANCES
335

ASSISTS
61

DRIBBLES
1199

PASSES
17158

SUCCESSFUL PASSES
84%

PENALTIES SCORED
10

GOALS
65

SHOTS
782

CHANCES CREATED
454

TACKLES
608

MAJOR CLUB HONOURS
⚽ Serie A: x 4 between 2013 and 2016 (Juventus)
⚽ UEFA Europa League: 2017
⚽ Coppa Italia: 2015, 2016 (Juventus)

INTERNATIONAL HONOURS
⚽ FIFA World Cup: 2018

ACTIVITY AREAS

RENATO SANCHES

Renato Sanches can play in almost every midfield position: defensive, wide, central or as a creative playmaker. Calm in possession, he is a fine passer, strong tackler and isn't afraid of shooting from distance.

NATIONALITY
Portuguese

CURRENT CLUB
Lille

BIRTHDATE	18/08/1997
POSITION	CENTRAL
HEIGHT	1.76 M
WEIGHT	70 KG
PREFERRED FOOT	RIGHT

APPEARANCES
112

ASSISTS
3

DRIBBLES
308

PASSES
3702

SUCCESSFUL
PASSES
87%

PENALTIES
SCORED
0

GOALS
6

SHOTS
109

CHANCES
CREATED
78

TACKLES
87

MAJOR CLUB HONOURS
⚽ Bundesliga: 2017, 2019 (Bayern Munich)

INTERNATIONAL HONOURS
⚽ UEFA European Championship: 2016

ACTIVITY AREAS

NATIONALITY
South Korean

CURRENT CLUB
Tottenham Hotspur

SON HEUNG-MIN

Son Heung-Min is at his best when he plays behind the main striker. Although excellent with both feet, attacking from the right side is his strength and he converts a lot of chances that are set up by knock-downs or passes across the box.

BIRTHDATE	08/07/1992
POSITION	WINGER
HEIGHT	1.83 M
WEIGHT	78 KG
PREFERRED FOOT	BOTH

APPEARANCES
387

ASSISTS
55

DRIBBLES
1190

PASSES
8833

SUCCESSFUL PASSES
81%

PENALTIES SCORED
0

GOALS
130

SHOTS
830

CHANCES CREATED
406

TACKLES
326

MAJOR CLUB HONOURS
⚽ UEFA Champions League: runner-up 2019

INTERNATIONAL HONOURS
⚽ AFC Asian Cup: runner-up 2015

ACTIVITY AREAS

MARCO VERRATTI

Marco Verratti is an awesome ball-playing midfielder. He is able to dribble past defenders at speed to set up chances for the players ahead of him. He can pass or shoot accurately and powerfully with both feet.

NATIONALITY
Italian

CURRENT CLUB
Paris Saint-Germain

BIRTHDATE	05/11/1992
POSITION	CENTRAL
HEIGHT	1.65 M
WEIGHT	60 KG
PREFERRED FOOT	RIGHT

APPEARANCES
285

ASSISTS
44

DRIBBLES
549

PASSES
23301
SUCCESSFUL PASSES
91%

PENALTIES SCORED
0

GOALS
8

SHOTS
85

CHANCES CREATED
313

TACKLES
783

MAJOR CLUB HONOURS
- ⚽ Ligue 1: 2013, 2014, 2015, 2016, 2018, 2019, 2020
- ⚽ UEFA Champions League: runner-up 2020
- ⚽ Coupe de France: 2015, 2016, 2017, 2018, 2020

INTERNATIONAL HONOURS
- ⚽ None to date

ACTIVITY AREAS

NATIONALITY
Dutch

CURRENT CLUB
Liverpool

GEORGINIO WIJNALDUM

Georginio Wijnaldum can play anywhere in the middle of the pitch as an attacking playmaker or a defensive shield for the back-line. Good with both feet and a strong tackler, he goes box to box and scores crucial goals, especially with headers.

BIRTHDATE	11/11/1990
POSITION	ATTACKING
HEIGHT	1.75 M
WEIGHT	69 KG
PREFERRED FOOT	RIGHT

ASSISTS
18

APPEARANCES
276

DRIBBLES
520

PASSES
11347

SUCCESSFUL
PASSES
89%

PENALTIES
SCORED
2

GOALS
39

SHOTS
322

CHANCES
CREATED
221

TACKLES
287

MAJOR CLUB HONOURS

⚽ Premier League: 2020
⚽ UEFA Champions League: 2019, runner-up 2018
⚽ UEFA Super Cup: 2019
⚽ FIFA Club World Cup: 2019

INTERNATIONAL HONOURS

⚽ UEFA Nations League: runner-up: 2019
⚽ FIFA World Cup: third place 2014

ACTIVITY AREAS

AXEL WITSEL

Originally a pacy right-winger, Axel Witsel has developed into a strong central midfielder for his club. He frequently drives his team forward with both his play and leadership skills. He is especially good at delivering dangerous passes with either foot.

NATIONALITY
Belgian

CURRENT CLUB
Borussia Dortmund

28

BIRTHDATE	12/01/1989
POSITION	CENTRAL
HEIGHT	1.86 M
WEIGHT	81 KG
PREFERRED FOOT	RIGHT

APPEARANCES 168
ASSISTS 10
DRIBBLES 197
PENALTIES SCORED 1
PASSES 9680
SUCCESSFUL PASSES 91%
GOALS 18
SHOTS 181
CHANCES CREATED 96
TACKLES 291

MAJOR CLUB HONOURS
⚽ DFL-Supercup: 2019

INTERNATIONAL HONOURS
⚽ FIFA World Cup: third place 2018

ACTIVITY AREAS

FORWARDS

The forwards, or strikers, are a team's frontline attackers and the chief goalscorers. They are also the team's most celebrated players. Whether it is the smaller, quicker player, such as Neymar Jr and Mohamed Salah, or the bigger, more physical attacker, such as Cristiano Ronaldo and Romelu Lukaku, strikers have perfected the ability to find the back of the net on a regular basis. Aside from scoring lots of goals the world's best strikers are also effective in creating chances for their team-mates.

WHAT DO THE STATS MEAN?

GOALS

This is the total number of goals a striker has scored. The figure spans across all the top clubs the player has represented so far in their career.

CONVERSION RATE

The percentage shows how good the player is at taking their chance in front of goal - if a player scores two goals from four shots, their conversion rate is 50%.

ASSISTS

A pass, cross or header to a team-mate who then scores counts as an assist. This stat also includes a deflected shot that is immediately converted by a team-mate.

MINUTES PER GOAL

This is the average length of time it takes for the player to score. It is calculated across all the minutes the player has played in their career at top level.

Did you know?

A perfect hat-trick is one where the player scores one goal with his right foot, another with his left foot and a third with his head. It does not matter in which order the goals come.

NATIONALITY
Argentinian

CURRENT CLUB
Manchester City

SERGIO AGÜERO

Sergio Agüero is one of the most complete strikers in world football today. Good coming in from either wing or down the centre, he can beat defenders on the dribble or with his pace, then shoot powerfully and accurately with either foot.

BIRTHDATE	02/06/1988
POSITION	STRIKER
HEIGHT	1.73 M
WEIGHT	70 KG
PREFERRED FOOT	RIGHT

GOALS 311
PENALTIES SCORED 40
ASSISTS 86
APPEARANCES 545
CONVERSION RATE 18%
MINUTES PER GOAL 128
GOALS LEFT 53
GOALS RIGHT 224
HAT-TRICKS 16
HEADED GOALS 29
SHOTS 1720

MAJOR CLUB HONOURS
- Premier League: 2012, 2014, 2018, 2019
- UEFA Europa League: 2010 (Atlético Madrid)
- UEFA Super Cup: 2010 (Atlético Madrid)
- FA Cup: 2019

INTERNATIONAL HONOURS
- Olympic Games: gold medal 2008
- FIFA World Cup: runner-up 2014
- Copa América: runner-up 2015, 2016

ACTIVITY AREAS

60

PIERRE-EMERICK AUBAMEYANG

Pierre-Emerick Aubameyang not only leads the line as a striker, but he is a great team leader as captain. He often beats the opposition defence with his speed and off-the-ball movement, and is lethal in front of goal.

NATIONALITY
Gabonese

CURRENT CLUB
Arsenal

14

BIRTHDATE	18/06/1989
POSITION	STRIKER
HEIGHT	1.87 M
WEIGHT	80 KG
PREFERRED FOOT	RIGHT

GOALS
239

PENALTIES SCORED
20

ASSISTS
56

APPEARANCES
446

CONVERSION RATE
19%

MINUTES PER GOAL
144

GOALS LEFT
40

GOALS RIGHT
172

HAT-TRICKS
9

HEADED GOALS
26

SHOTS
1270

MAJOR CLUB HONOURS
- FA Cup: 2020
- UEFA Europa League: runner-up 2019
- DFB-Pokal: 2017 (Borussia Dortmund)

INTERNATIONAL HONOURS
- King's Cup: third place 2018

ACTIVITY AREAS

NATIONALITY
French

CURRENT CLUB
Real Madrid

KARIM BENZEMA

Karim Benzema is both a creator and scorer of goals. Intelligent with a great work-rate, he can play out wide, down the middle or behind the front man, and although right-footed, scores many goals with his left and his head.

BIRTHDATE	19/12/1987
POSITION	STRIKER
HEIGHT	1.85 M
WEIGHT	81 KG
PREFERRED FOOT	BOTH

GOALS
300

PENALTIES SCORED
13

ASSISTS
122

APPEARANCES
613

CONVERSION RATE
18%

MINUTES PER GOAL
143

GOALS LEFT
60

GOALS RIGHT
186

HAT-TRICKS
5

HEADED GOALS
50

SHOTS
1678

MAJOR CLUB HONOURS

⚽ La Liga: 2012, 2017, 2020 ⚽ FIFA Club World Cup: 2014, 2016, 2017, 2018 ⚽ UEFA Super Cup: 2014, 2016, 2017 ⚽ UEFA Champions League: 2014, 2016, 2017, 2018 ⚽ Ligue 1: 2005, 2006, 2007, 2008 (Lyon)

INTERNATIONAL HONOURS

⚽ UEFA European U-17 Championship: 2004

ACTIVITY AREAS

EDINSON CAVANI

Edinson Cavani is a fine dribbler, great at running into space and scoring spectacular goals, especially with overhead kicks. He has an impressive work rate, too, always hassling the opposition's defence to win the ball.

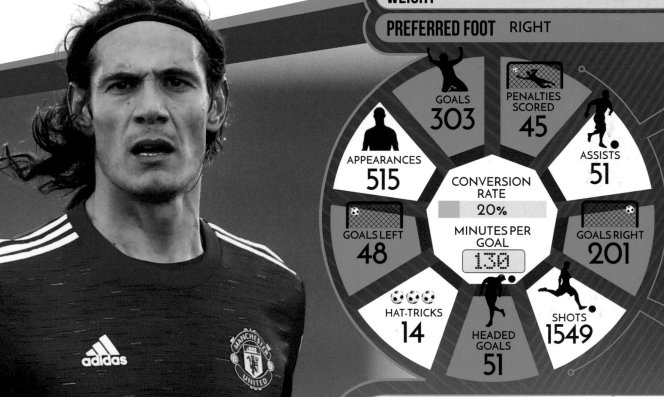

NATIONALITY
Uruguayan

CURRENT CLUB
Manchester United

BIRTHDATE	14/02/1987
POSITION	STRIKER
HEIGHT	1.84 M
WEIGHT	71 KG
PREFERRED FOOT	RIGHT

GOALS
303

PENALTIES SCORED
45

ASSISTS
51

APPEARANCES
515

CONVERSION RATE
20%

MINUTES PER GOAL
130

GOALS RIGHT
201

GOALS LEFT
48

HAT-TRICKS
14

HEADED GOALS
51

SHOTS
1549

MAJOR CLUB HONOURS
- Ligue 1: 2014, 2015, 2016, 2018, 2019 (PSG)
- Coupe de France: 2015, 2016, 2018, 2019 (PSG)
- Coppa Italia: 2012 (Napoli)

INTERNATIONAL HONOURS
- Copa América: 2011

ACTIVITY AREAS

63

NATIONALITY
Dutch

CURRENT CLUB
Olympique Lyonnais

MEMPHIS DEPAY

Memphis Depay has developed into a world-class striker, though he is still considered to be a left-winger or left-sided striker. Not very tall, he is very brave and will challenge the biggest defenders in the middle of the danger area.

BIRTHDATE	13/02/1994
POSITION	WINGER
HEIGHT	1.76 M
WEIGHT	78 KG
PREFERRED FOOT	RIGHT

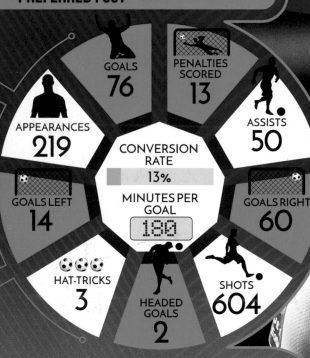

GOALS
76

PENALTIES SCORED
13

ASSISTS
50

APPEARANCES
219

CONVERSION RATE
13%

MINUTES PER GOAL
180

GOALS LEFT
14

GOALS RIGHT
60

HAT-TRICKS
3

HEADED GOALS
2

SHOTS
604

MAJOR CLUB HONOURS
⚽ Eredivisie: 2015 (PSV Eindhoven)
⚽ KNVB Cup: 2012 (PSV Eindhoven)

INTERNATIONAL HONOURS
⚽ FIFA World Cup: third place 2014

ACTIVITY AREAS

JOÃO FÉLIX

The latest great young striker to emerge out of Portugal, João Félix has developed into a regular goalscorer in La Liga. His tactical intelligence, energy and versatility mean he can be very effective as a central striker, second forward, attacking midfielder or winger.

NATIONALITY
Portuguese

CURRENT CLUB
Atlético Madrid

BIRTHDATE	10/11/1999
POSITION	FORWARD
HEIGHT	1.81 M
WEIGHT	70 KG
PREFERRED FOOT	RIGHT

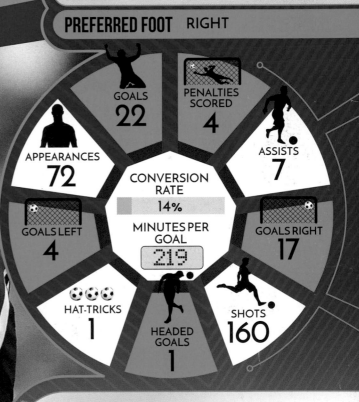

GOALS 22
PENALTIES SCORED 4
ASSISTS 7
APPEARANCES 72
CONVERSION RATE 14%
MINUTES PER GOAL 219
GOALS LEFT 4
GOALS RIGHT 17
HAT-TRICKS 1
HEADED GOALS 1
SHOTS 160

MAJOR CLUB HONOURS
⚽ Primeira Liga: 2019 (Benfica)

INTERNATIONAL HONOURS
⚽ UEFA Nations League: 2019

ACTIVITY AREAS

65

9

NATIONALITY
Norwegian

CURRENT CLUB
Borussia Dortmund

ERLING HAALAND

Erling Haaland has become one of the most exciting and promising forwards in world football. He has all the talents: two good feet, blistering pace, good in the air, energy, strength, timing and the instincts to get into scoring positions.

BIRTHDATE	21/07/2000
POSITION	STRIKER
HEIGHT	1.94 M
WEIGHT	88 KG
PREFERRED FOOT	LEFT

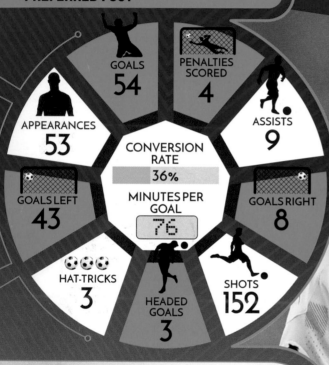

GOALS
54

PENALTIES SCORED
4

APPEARANCES
53

ASSISTS
9

CONVERSION RATE
36%

MINUTES PER GOAL
76

GOALS LEFT
43

GOALS RIGHT
8

HAT-TRICKS
3

HEADED GOALS
3

SHOTS
152

MAJOR CLUB HONOURS
- ⚽ Austrian Bundesliga: 2019, 2020 (Red Bull Salzburg)
- ⚽ Austrian Cup: 2019 (Red Bull Salzburg)

INTERNATIONAL HONOURS
- ⚽ FIFA U-20 World Cup: 2011
- ⚽ Copa América: 2019

ACTIVITY AREAS

ZLATAN IBRAHIMOVIĆ

 **NATIONALITY**
Swedish

CURRENT CLUB
AC Milan

Zlatan Ibrahimović is one of world football's most recognisable strikers. He is supremely self-confident, amazingly agile — overhead scissors kicks are a trademark — and he scores with either foot or head, from close in, long range, set pieces and open play.

BIRTHDATE	03/10/1981
POSITION	STRIKER
HEIGHT	1.95 M
WEIGHT	95 KG
PREFERRED FOOT	RIGHT

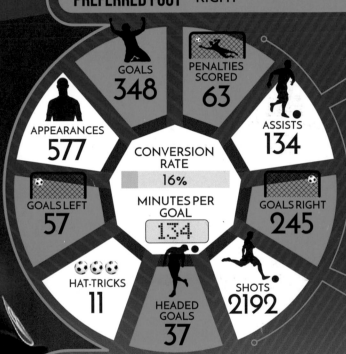

GOALS
348

PENALTIES SCORED
63

APPEARANCES
577

ASSISTS
134

CONVERSION RATE
16%

GOALS LEFT
57

MINUTES PER GOAL
134

GOALS RIGHT
245

HAT-TRICKS
11

HEADED GOALS
37

SHOTS
2192

MAJOR CLUB HONOURS
⚽ Serie A: 2007, 2008, 2009 (Inter Milan), 2011 (AC Milan)
⚽ La Liga: 2010 (Barcelona) ⚽ FIFA Club World Cup: 2009 (Barcelona) ⚽ UEFA Europa League: 2017 (Man Utd) ⚽ Ligue 1: 2013, 2014, 2015, 2016 (PSG)

INTERNATIONAL HONOURS
⚽ None to date

ACTIVITY AREAS

NATIONALITY
Italian

CURRENT CLUB
Lazio

CIRO IMMOBILE

A great team-player, Ciro Immobile is a natural finisher who is excellent in the air. His goals tally is even higher because he refuses to give up lost causes and is willing to chase back to force mistakes out of defenders.

BIRTHDATE	20/02/1990
POSITION	STRIKER
HEIGHT	1.85 M
WEIGHT	78 KG
PREFERRED FOOT	RIGHT

GOALS
174

PENALTIES SCORED
40

APPEARANCES
316

ASSISTS
45

CONVERSION RATE
19%

GOALS LEFT
23

MINUTES PER GOAL
132

GOALS RIGHT
134

HAT-TRICKS
6

HEADED GOALS
17

SHOTS
930

MAJOR CLUB HONOURS
⚽ Coppa Italia: 2019 (Lazio)

INTERNATIONAL HONOURS
⚽ UEFA European U-21 Championship: runner-up 2013

ACTIVITY AREAS

LUKA JOVIĆ

Luka Jović is a predator in the penalty box. He uses his speed and attacking instincts to find spaces in the penalty area and score goals from close range with deft touches from either foot and, occasionally, his head.

NATIONALITY
Serbian

CURRENT CLUB
Eintracht Frankfurt

BIRTHDATE	23/12/1997
POSITION	STRIKER
HEIGHT	1.82 M
WEIGHT	85 KG
PREFERRED FOOT	RIGHT

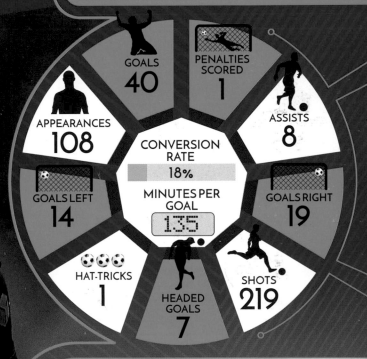

GOALS
40

PENALTIES SCORED
1

ASSISTS
8

APPEARANCES
108

CONVERSION RATE
18%

MINUTES PER GOAL
135

GOALS LEFT
14

GOALS RIGHT
19

HAT-TRICKS
1

HEADED GOALS
7

SHOTS
219

MAJOR CLUB HONOURS
- La Liga: 2020 (Real Madrid)
- DFB-Pokal: 2018

INTERNATIONAL HONOURS
- None to date

ACTIVITY AREAS

69

CURRENT CLUB
Tottenham Hotspur

HARRY KANE

Harry Kane has developed his game to become a complete striker. His great pace, power in the air, physical strength and technical ability with both feet, make him hard to stop and he sets up many goals for his team-mates.

BIRTHDATE	28/07/1993
POSITION	STRIKER
HEIGHT	1.88 M
WEIGHT	86 KG
PREFERRED FOOT	RIGHT

GOALS
193

PENALTIES SCORED
27

ASSISTS
41

APPEARANCES
293

CONVERSION RATE
18%

MINUTES PER GOAL
121

GOALS RIGHT
117

GOALS LEFT
40

HAT-TRICKS
10

HEADED GOALS
35

SHOTS
1060

MAJOR CLUB HONOURS
⚽ UEFA Champions League: runner-up 2019

INTERNATIONAL HONOURS
⚽ UEFA Nations League: third place 2019

ACTIVITY AREAS

ROBERT LEWANDOWSKI

NATIONALITY
Polish

CURRENT CLUB
Bayern Munich

Robert Lewandowski has consistently ranked as one of the world's best strikers ever since he made his debut at Borussia Dortmund in 2010. His positioning, technique, power and finishing have seen him net more than 275 goals for Bayern.

BIRTHDATE	21/08/1988
POSITION	STRIKER
HEIGHT	1.84 M
WEIGHT	80 KG
PREFERRED FOOT	RIGHT

GOALS
346

PENALTIES SCORED
46

APPEARANCES
456

ASSISTS
68

CONVERSION RATE
20%

MINUTES PER GOAL
106

GOALS LEFT
55

GOALS RIGHT
229

HAT-TRICKS
16

HEADED GOALS
58

SHOTS
1723

MAJOR CLUB HONOURS
⚽ Bundesliga: 2011, 2012 (Borussia Dortmund), 2015, 2016, 2017, 2018, 2019, 2020 ⚽ UEFA Champions League: 2020 ⚽ DFB-Pokal: 2012 (Borussia Dortmund), 2016, 2019, 2020 ⚽ FIFA Club World Cup: 2021

INTERNATIONAL HONOURS
⚽ None to date

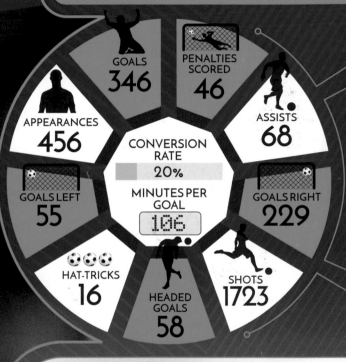

ACTIVITY AREAS

NATIONALITY
Belgian

CURRENT CLUB
Inter Milan

ROMELU LUKAKU

Romelu Lukaku often uses his size and strength to dispossess defenders before controlling the ball and unleashing a fierce shot or a pass to a well-placed team-mate. He is also superb in the air and scores many headers.

BIRTHDATE	13/05/1993
POSITION	STRIKER
HEIGHT	1.90 M
WEIGHT	94 KG
PREFERRED FOOT	LEFT

GOALS
190

PENALTIES SCORED
21

ASSISTS
55

APPEARANCES
376

CONVERSION RATE
19%

MINUTES PER GOAL
151

GOALS LEFT
106

GOALS RIGHT
47

HAT-TRICKS
4

HEADED GOALS
35

SHOTS
1005

MAJOR CLUB HONOURS
⚽ UEFA Europa League: runner-up 2020
⚽ Belgian Pro League: 2010 (Anderlecht)

INTERNATIONAL HONOURS
⚽ FIFA World Cup: third place 2018

ACTIVITY AREAS

SADIO MANÉ

Sadio Mané has breathtaking pace and dribbling ability. Although he normally plays on the wing, he can also be dangerous in the middle of the park as he can leap high to win headers and shoot powerfully with either foot.

NATIONALITY
Senegalese

CURRENT CLUB
Liverpool

BIRTHDATE	10/04/1992
POSITION	WINGER
HEIGHT	1.75 M
WEIGHT	69 KG
PREFERRED FOOT	RIGHT

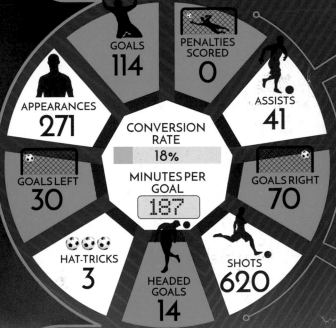

GOALS
114

PENALTIES SCORED
0

ASSISTS
41

APPEARANCES
271

CONVERSION RATE
18%

MINUTES PER GOAL
187

GOALS LEFT
30

GOALS RIGHT
70

HAT-TRICKS
3

HEADED GOALS
14

SHOTS
620

MAJOR CLUB HONOURS
- Premier League: 2020
- UEFA Champions League: 2019, runner-up 2018
- UEFA Super Cup: 2019
- FIFA Club World Cup: 2019

INTERNATIONAL HONOURS
- CAF Africa Cup of Nations: runner-up 2019

ACTIVITY AREAS

7

NATIONALITY
French

CURRENT CLUB
Paris Saint-Germain

KYLIAN MBAPPÉ

A FIFA World Cup winner with France at just 18, Kylian Mbappé may well be the best young striker in world football at the moment. He is a superb ball-player who consistently gets on the score sheet and sets up chances for team-mates.

BIRTHDATE	20/12/1998
POSITION	STRIKER
HEIGHT	1.78 M
WEIGHT	73 KG
PREFERRED FOOT	RIGHT

GOALS
127

PENALTIES SCORED
8

APPEARANCES
187

ASSISTS
52

CONVERSION RATE
23%

MINUTES PER GOAL
103

GOALS LEFT
27

GOALS RIGHT
95

HAT-TRICKS
6

HEADED GOALS
5

SHOTS
558

MAJOR CLUB HONOURS
- ⚽ Ligue 1: 2017 (Monaco), 2018, 2019, 2020
- ⚽ UEFA Champions League: runner-up 2020
- ⚽ Coupe de France: 2018, 2020

INTERNATIONAL HONOURS
- ⚽ FIFA World Cup: 2018

ACTIVITY AREAS

LIONEL MESSI

The greatest player of his generation, if not the greatest ever, Lionel Messi is a fine playmaker with a stunning goal-scoring record. He is also a fantastically fast dribbler who can carve out opportunities to shoot with either foot, from any range.

NATIONALITY
Argentinian

CURRENT CLUB
Barcelona

BIRTHDATE	24/06/1987
POSITION	FORWARD
HEIGHT	1.70 M
WEIGHT	72 KG
PREFERRED FOOT	LEFT

GOALS
587

PENALTIES SCORED
76

APPEARANCES
661

ASSISTS
226

CONVERSION RATE
20%

GOALS LEFT
485

MINUTES PER GOAL
92

GOALS RIGHT
82

HAT-TRICKS
44

HEADED GOALS
19

SHOTS
2985

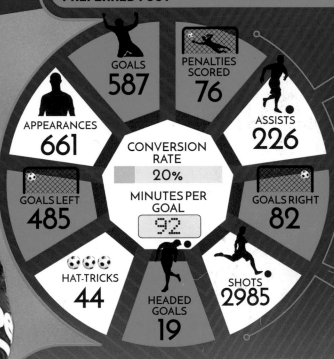

MAJOR CLUB HONOURS
⚽ La Liga: 2005, 2006, 2009, 2010, 2011, 2013, 2015, 2016, 2018, 2019 ⚽ UEFA Champions League: 2006, 2009, 2011, 2015 ⚽ UEFA Super Cup: 2009, 2011, 2015 ⚽ FIFA Club World Cup: 2009, 2011, 2015

INTERNATIONAL HONOURS
⚽ FIFA World Cup: runner-up 2014
⚽ Olympic Games: gold medal 2008
⚽ Copa América: runner-up 2015, 2016

ACTIVITY AREAS

9

NATIONALITY
Spanish

CURRENT CLUB
Juventus

ÁLVARO MORATA

Álvaro Morata is perfectly built for a central striker. Tall, strong and excellent in the air, he is comfortable with the ball at his feet. Morata is also surprisingly fast and has great tactical and positional awareness.

BIRTHDATE	23/10/1992
POSITION	STRIKER
HEIGHT	1.90 M
WEIGHT	84 KG
PREFERRED FOOT	RIGHT

GOALS 104

PENALTIES SCORED 4

APPEARANCES 310

ASSISTS 42

CONVERSION RATE 17%

MINUTES PER GOAL 157

GOALS LEFT 22

GOALS RIGHT 52

HAT-TRICKS 2

HEADED GOALS 30

SHOTS 597

MAJOR CLUB HONOURS

⚽ La Liga: 2012, 2017 (Real Madrid) ⚽ Serie A: 2015, 2016 ⚽ UEFA Champions League: 2014, 2017 (Real Madrid) ⚽ UEFA Super Cup: 2016 (Real Madrid) ⚽ FIFA Club World Cup: 2016 (Real Madrid)

INTERNATIONAL HONOURS

⚽ UEFA European U-21 Championship: 2013

ACTIVITY AREAS

NEYMAR JR

Great Brazilian strikers have a lot to live up to, and Neymar does that, leading the attack and taking and making chances. An emotional leader, he is good with both feet, has superb ball control, attacking instincts and football intelligence.

NATIONALITY
Brazilian

CURRENT CLUB
Paris Saint-Germain

BIRTHDATE	05/02/1992
POSITION	WINGER
HEIGHT	1.75 M
WEIGHT	68 KG
PREFERRED FOOT	RIGHT

GOALS
162

PENALTIES SCORED
27

APPEARANCES
254

ASSISTS
93

CONVERSION RATE
18%

MINUTES PER GOAL
131

GOALS LEFT
45

GOALS RIGHT
111

HAT-TRICKS
7

HEADED GOALS
6

SHOTS
878

MAJOR CLUB HONOURS
⚽ La Liga: 2015, 2016, 2017 (Barcelona) ⚽ Ligue 1: 2018, 2019, 2020 ⚽ UEFA Champions League: 2016 (Barcelona) ⚽ FIFA Club World Cup: 2016 (Barcelona) ⚽ Coupe de France: 2018, 2020 ⚽ Copa Libertadores: 2011 (Santos)

INTERNATIONAL HONOURS
⚽ FIFA Confederations Cup: 2013
⚽ Olympic Games: silver medal 2012, gold medal 2016

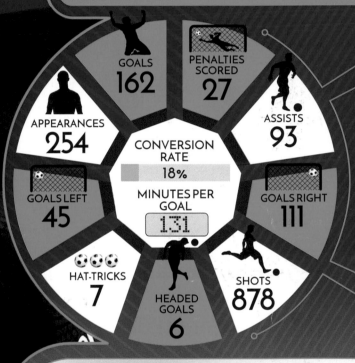

ACTIVITY AREAS

11

NATIONALITY
German

CURRENT CLUB
Borussia Dortmund

MARCO REUS

Marco Reus is an attacker who can lead the front line, play as a second striker or out wide. He is an expert finisher, especially with his right foot, and is also fantastic at setting up chances for his team-mates.

BIRTHDATE	31/05/1989
POSITION	FORWARD
HEIGHT	1.80 M
WEIGHT	71 KG
PREFERRED FOOT	RIGHT

GOALS
153

PENALTIES SCORED
14

APPEARANCES
367

ASSISTS
85

CONVERSION RATE
16%

GOALS LEFT
34

MINUTES PER GOAL
188

GOALS RIGHT
113

HAT-TRICKS
3

HEADED GOALS
6

SHOTS
932

MAJOR CLUB HONOURS
⚽ UEFA Champions League: runner-up 2013
⚽ DFB-Pokal: 2017

INTERNATIONAL HONOURS
⚽ None to date

ACTIVITY AREAS

CRISTIANO RONALDO

The superstar striker has wowed fans across the world with his all-round attacking skills. He is breathtaking to watch when he is running at defences, brilliant in the air and a superb finisher, with an extraordinary goal-scoring record.

NATIONALITY
Portuguese

CURRENT CLUB
Juventus

BIRTHDATE	05/02/1985
POSITION	FORWARD
HEIGHT	1.87 M
WEIGHT	83 KG
PREFERRED FOOT	RIGHT

GOALS
606

PENALTIES SCORED
113

APPEARANCES
756

ASSISTS
177

CONVERSION RATE
14%

MINUTES PER GOAL
104

GOALS LEFT
104

GOALS RIGHT
401

HAT-TRICKS
45

HEADED GOALS
99

SHOTS
4325

MAJOR CLUB HONOURS

⚽ Serie A: 2019, 2020 ⚽ EPL: 2007, 2008, 2009 (Man U)
⚽ La Liga: 2012, 2017 (R Mad) ⚽ UEFA Champ League:
2008 (Man U), 2014, 2016, 2017, 2018 (R Mad) ⚽ FIFA Club
World Cup: 2008 (Man U), 2014, 2016, 2017 (R Mad)

INTERNATIONAL HONOURS

⚽ UEFA European Championship: 2016
⚽ UEFA Nations League: 2019

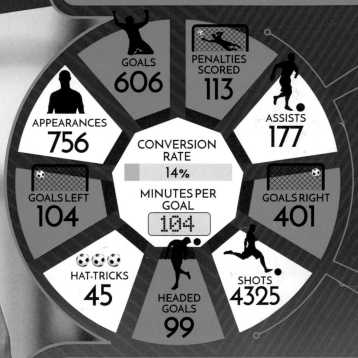

ACTIVITY AREAS

11

NATIONALITY
Egyptian

CURRENT CLUB
Liverpool

MOHAMED SALAH

The two-time African Footballer of the Year is a brilliant left-footed attacker who prowls the left wing. Mo Salah has amazing pace with the ability to make angled runs, finding gaps in defences before scoring spectacular goals.

BIRTHDATE	15/06/1992
POSITION	WINGER
HEIGHT	1.75 M
WEIGHT	71 KG
PREFERRED FOOT	LEFT

GOALS **161**

PENALTIES SCORED **16**

APPEARANCES **316**

ASSISTS **66**

CONVERSION RATE **17%**

MINUTES PER GOAL **154**

GOALS LEFT **129**

GOALS RIGHT **26**

HAT-TRICKS **4**

HEADED GOALS **6**

SHOTS **951**

MAJOR CLUB HONOURS
⚽ Premier League: 2020
⚽ UEFA Champions League: 2019, runner-up 2018
⚽ UEFA Super Cup: 2019
⚽ FIFA Club World Cup: 2019

INTERNATIONAL HONOURS
⚽ CAF Africa Cup of Nations: runner-up 2017

ACTIVITY AREAS

RAHEEM STERLING

Raheem Sterling has become the complete forward at Manchester City. No longer a winger, he plays all over the front line, but is better behind a front man, coming off the left side and firing unstoppable shots with his preferred right foot.

NATIONALITY
English

CURRENT CLUB
Manchester City

BIRTHDATE	08/12/1994
POSITION	FORWARD
HEIGHT	1.70 M
WEIGHT	69 KG
PREFERRED FOOT	RIGHT

GOALS
116

PENALTIES SCORED
1

APPEARANCES
352

ASSISTS
64

CONVERSION RATE
16%

MINUTES PER GOAL
225

GOALS LEFT
30

GOALS RIGHT
78

HAT-TRICKS
5

HEADED GOALS
8

SHOTS
716

MAJOR CLUB HONOURS
⚽ Premier League: 2018, 2019
⚽ FA Cup: 2019

INTERNATIONAL HONOURS
⚽ UEFA Europa Nations League: third place 2019

ACTIVITY AREAS

NATIONALITY
Uruguayan

CURRENT CLUB
Atlético Madrid

LUIS SUÁREZ

Luis Suárez has a talent for scoring spectacular goals with his right foot, either facing or with his back to goal. He loves running at defenders and beating them with pace or dribbling trickery before smashing great shots past goalkeepers.

BIRTHDATE	24/01/1987
POSITION	FORWARD
HEIGHT	1.82 M
WEIGHT	86 KG
PREFERRED FOOT	RIGHT

GOALS **272**
PENALTIES SCORED **16**
ASSISTS **119**
APPEARANCES **420**
CONVERSION RATE **17%**
MINUTES PER GOAL **130**
GOALS LEFT **53**
GOALS RIGHT **189**
HAT-TRICKS **16**
HEADED GOALS **28**
SHOTS **1580**

MAJOR CLUB HONOURS
⚽ La Liga: 2015, 2016, 2018, 2019 (Barcelona) ⚽ UEFA Champions League: 2015 (Barcelona) ⚽ UEFA Super Cup: 2015 (Barcelona) ⚽ FIFA Club World Cup: 2015 (Barcelona) ⚽ Copa del Rey: 2015, 2016, 2017, 2018 (Barcelona)

INTERNATIONAL HONOURS
⚽ Copa América 2011

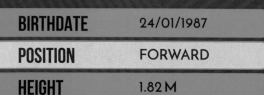

ACTIVITY AREAS

JAMIE VARDY

Jamie Vardy came late into top-flight football and is still getting better. Mainly right-footed, he is an old-fashioned goal-scoring No. 9, leading the line with his strength, power and bravery, beating defenders in the air and on the ground.

NATIONALITY
English

CURRENT CLUB
Leicester City

BIRTHDATE	11/01/1987
POSITION	STRIKER
HEIGHT	1.79 M
WEIGHT	74 KG
PREFERRED FOOT	RIGHT

GOALS
119

PENALTIES SCORED
25

ASSISTS
36

APPEARANCES
250

CONVERSION RATE
22%

MINUTES PER GOAL
171

GOALS LEFT
29

GOALS RIGHT
77

HAT-TRICKS
3

HEADED GOALS
13

SHOTS
539

MAJOR CLUB HONOURS
⚽ Premier League: 2016

INTERNATIONAL HONOURS
⚽ None to date

ACTIVITY AREAS

GOALKEEPERS

The goalkeeper is a team's last line of defence and unlike the other positions there is no one playing next to them. There is more pressure on goalkeepers than in any other position because when a keeper makes an error, the chances are that the other team will score. The goalies featured in this section are all great shot-stoppers, but some play outside their penalty areas as sweeper-keepers; others have made their reputation as penalty-savers; then there are the keepers who are great at catching the ball or punching it clear.

WHAT DO THE STATS MEAN?

 ### CATCHES
This is the number of times the keeper has dealt with a dangerous ball – usually a cross – by catching the ball.

 ### PENALTIES FACED/SAVED
This is the number of times a goalie has faced a penalty (excludes shoot-outs) and how successful they have been at saving it.

 ### CLEAN SHEETS
Any occasion on which the goalie has not let in a goal for the full duration of the game counts as a clean sheet.

 ### PUNCHES
This is a measure of how often the keeper has dealt with a dangerous ball (usually a cross) by punching it clear.

 ### GOALS CONCEDED
This is the number of goals the keeper has conceded in their career in top-division football.

 ### SAVES
This shows how many times the goalkeeper has stopped a shot or header that was on target.

Did you **know?**

Goalkeepers can, in theory, score goals with their hands. If they throw a ball downfield and it goes directly into the opposition net, the goal will count but, of course, the ball would have to travel more than 90 metres.

NATIONALITY
Brazilian

CURRENT CLUB
Liverpool

ALISSON

The Brazilian has proved to be a top keeper at Liverpool. Alisson is a superb shot-stopper and great at dealing with crosses. Incredibly quick off his line to foil any threat, he can turn defence into attack by finding team-mates with long or short passes.

BIRTHDATE	02/10/1992
POSITION	GOALKEEPER
HEIGHT	1.91 M
WEIGHT	91 KG
PREFERRED FOOT	RIGHT

GOALS CONCEDED
152

APPEARANCES
175

PENALTIES SAVED
3

CLEAN SHEETS
77

SAVES
464

PENALTIES FACED
15

CATCHES
55

PUNCHES
62

MAJOR CLUB HONOURS
⚽ Premier League: 2020
⚽ UEFA Champions League: 2019
⚽ FIFA Club World Cup: 2019

INTERNATIONAL HONOURS
⚽ Copa América: 2019

ACTIVITY AREAS

BONO

Bono (Yassine Bounou) was born in Canada but represents Morocco, the country where he grew up. Very brave and quick to assess dangerous situations, he cuts down angles very well, is an outstanding shot-stopper and also a great communicator.

NATIONALITY
Moroccan

CURRENT CLUB
Sevilla

BIRTHDATE	05/04/1991
POSITION	GOALKEEPER
HEIGHT	1.92 M
WEIGHT	78 KG
PREFERRED FOOT	RIGHT

GOALS CONCEDED
120

APPEARANCES
108

PENALTIES SAVED
3

CLEAN SHEETS
41

SAVES
343

PENALTIES FACED
21

CATCHES
35

PUNCHES
35

MAJOR CLUB HONOURS
- UEFA Europa League: 2020
- La Liga: 2014 (Atlético Madrid)

INTERNATIONAL HONOURS
- None to date

ACTIVITY AREAS

NATIONALITY
Belgian

CURRENT CLUB
Real Madrid

THIBAUT COURTOIS

Thibaut Courtois uses his height to dominate his penalty area, catching crosses and punching well. An agile shot-stopper, he can get down low to make saves, communicates well with his defence, is excellent coming off his line and passes well.

BIRTHDATE	11/05/1992
POSITION	GOALKEEPER
HEIGHT	1.99 M
WEIGHT	96 KG
PREFERRED FOOT	LEFT

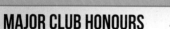

GOALS CONCEDED
363

APPEARANCES
390

PENALTIES SAVED
4

CLEAN SHEETS
165

SAVES
921

PENALTIES FACED
33

CATCHES
431

PUNCHES
124

MAJOR CLUB HONOURS

⚽ La Liga: 2014 (Atlético Madrid), 2020 ⚽ Premier League: 2015, 2017 (Chelsea) ⚽ UEFA Europa League: 2012 (Atlético Madrid) ⚽ FIFA Club World Cup: 2018 ⚽ UEFA Super Cup: 2012 (Atlético Madrid)

INTERNATIONAL HONOURS

⚽ FIFA World Cup: third place 2018

ACTIVITY AREAS

DAVID DE GEA

David De Gea is an effective keeper, though unorthodox at times (he is known for using his legs to make saves). Agile and athletic, he marshals his penalty area well. His catching has improved, but he is still happier punching the ball the clear.

NATIONALITY
Spanish

CURRENT CLUB
Manchester United

BIRTHDATE	07/11/1990
POSITION	GOALKEEPER
HEIGHT	1.92 M
WEIGHT	76 KG
PREFERRED FOOT	RIGHT

GOALS CONCEDED
507

APPEARANCES
467

PENALTIES SAVED
6

CLEAN SHEETS
158

SAVES
1354

PENALTIES FACED
47

CATCHES
323

PUNCHES
161

MAJOR CLUB HONOURS
- Premier League: 2013
- UEFA Europa League: 2010 (Atlético Madrid), 2017
- UEFA Super Cup: 2010 (Atlético Madrid)

INTERNATIONAL HONOURS
- None to date

ACTIVITY AREAS

89

NATIONALITY
Italian

CURRENT CLUB
AC Milan

GIANLUIGI DONNARUMMA

The Italian is an amazing talent who made his Serie A debut aged just 16 and won his first Italian cap at 17. Mentally strong and composed under pressure, he has everything it takes to become an all-time great.

BIRTHDATE	25/02/1999
POSITION	GOALKEEPER
HEIGHT	1.96 M
WEIGHT	90 KG
PREFERRED FOOT	RIGHT

GOALS CONCEDED
241

APPEARANCES
222

PENALTIES SAVED
8

CLEAN SHEETS
69

SAVES
637

PENALTIES FACED
36

CATCHES
146

PUNCHES
118

MAJOR CLUB HONOURS
⚽ Supercoppa Italiana: 2016

INTERNATIONAL HONOURS
⚽ None to date

ACTIVITY AREAS

EDERSON

Owing to his range of passing and great ball skills, Ederson is often considered a playmaker goalkeeper and counted as one of the best in the English Premier League. He is a fine shot-stopper with a reputation for being a great penalty-kick saver, too.

NATIONALITY
Brazilian

CURRENT CLUB
Manchester City

BIRTHDATE	17/08/1993
POSITION	GOALKEEPER
HEIGHT	1.88 M
WEIGHT	86 KG
PREFERRED FOOT	LEFT

GOALS CONCEDED
146

APPEARANCES
186

PENALTIES SAVED
5

CLEAN SHEETS
87

SAVES
359

PENALTIES FACED
26

CATCHES
82

PUNCHES
49

MAJOR CLUB HONOURS
⚽ Premier League: 2018, 2019
⚽ FA Cup: 2019

INTERNATIONAL HONOURS
⚽ Copa América: 2019

ACTIVITY AREAS

NATIONALITY
Hungarian

CURRENT CLUB
RB Leipzig

PÉTER GULÁCSI

Péter Gulácsi is dedicated to preparing for every football situation he faces. He studies approaching forwards to get an instinct for where they are going to shoot, gets into the right position and then makes difficult saves look very easy.

BIRTHDATE	06/05/1990
POSITION	GOALKEEPER
HEIGHT	1.91 M
WEIGHT	86 KG
PREFERRED FOOT	RIGHT

GOALS CONCEDED
241

APPEARANCES
205

PENALTIES SAVED
3

SAVES
509

CLEAN SHEETS
63

PENALTIES FACED
26

CATCHES
133

PUNCHES
59

MAJOR CLUB HONOURS
⚽ Austrian Bundesliga: 2014, 2015 (Red Bull Salzburg)
⚽ Austrian Cup: 2014, 2015 (Red Bull Salzburg)

INTERNATIONAL HONOURS
⚽ FIFA U-20 World Cup: third place 2009

ACTIVITY AREAS

92

EIJI KAWASHIMA

A goalkeeper who communicates well with his defenders, Eiji Kawashima's best asset is his ability to meet balls that seem way out of reach. His quick movement in the penalty area makes him good at anticipating and saving shots.

NATIONALITY
Japanese

CURRENT CLUB
Strasbourg

BIRTHDATE	20/03/1983
POSITION	GOALKEEPER
HEIGHT	1.85 M
WEIGHT	74 KG
PREFERRED FOOT	RIGHT

GOALS CONCEDED
96

APPEARANCES
57

PENALTIES SAVED
4

SAVES
187

CLEAN SHEETS
11

PENALTIES FACED
8

PUNCHES
15

CATCHES
15

MAJOR CLUB HONOURS
⚽ None to date

INTERNATIONAL HONOURS
⚽ AFC Asian Cup: 2011

ACTIVITY AREAS

93

CURRENT CLUB
Tottenham Hotspur

HUGO LLORIS

Hugo Lloris is a natural leader, good at organising his defence. Armed with excellent reflexes, he is brilliant at coming off his line to clear the danger and then distributing the ball quickly, which has earned him the sweeper-keeper label.

BIRTHDATE	26/12/1986
POSITION	GOALKEEPER
HEIGHT	1.88 M
WEIGHT	82 KG
PREFERRED FOOT	LEFT

GOALS CONCEDED
642

APPEARANCES
603

PENALTIES SAVED
10

CLEAN SHEETS
204

SAVES
1667

PENALTIES FACED
67

CATCHES
753

PUNCHES
388

MAJOR CLUB HONOURS
- UEFA Champions League: runner-up 2019
- Coupe de France: 2012 (Olympique Lyonnais)

INTERNATIONAL HONOURS
- FIFA World Cup: 2018

ACTIVITY AREAS

STEVE MANDANDA

After a brief stint in the Premier League, Steve Mandanda returned to Marseille, for whom he has made more than 500 appearances. His class and consistency have seen him win the Ligue 1 Goalkeeper of the Year award five times.

NATIONALITY
French

CURRENT CLUB
Marseille

BIRTHDATE	28/03/1985
POSITION	GOALKEEPER
HEIGHT	1.85 M
WEIGHT	82 KG
PREFERRED FOOT	RIGHT

GOALS CONCEDED
613

APPEARANCES
544

PENALTIES SAVED
13

CLEAN SHEETS
166

SAVES
1298

PENALTIES FACED
69

CATCHES
785

PUNCHES
215

MAJOR CLUB HONOURS
⚽ UEFA Europa League: runner-up 2018

INTERNATIONAL HONOURS
⚽ FIFA World Cup: 2018

ACTIVITY AREAS

NATIONALITY
Senegalese

CURRENT CLUB
Chelsea

ÉDOUARD MENDY

French-born Édouard Mendy dominates his penalty area, both physically and vocally, marshalling his defence very well, dealing with aerial threats and is among the best in shot-stopping and ball distribution statistics.

BIRTHDATE	01/03/1992
POSITION	GOALKEEPER
HEIGHT	1.97 M
WEIGHT	86 KG
PREFERRED FOOT	RIGHT

GOALS CONCEDED
90

APPEARANCES
100

PENALTIES SAVED
1

SAVES
249

CLEAN SHEETS
44

PENALTIES FACED
14

CATCHES
67

PUNCHES
28

MAJOR CLUB HONOURS
⚽ None to date

INTERNATIONAL HONOURS
⚽ CAF Africa Cup of Nations: runner-up 2019

ACTIVITY AREAS

KEYLOR NAVAS

After fantastic performances at the 2014 FIFA World Cup, Keylor Navas earned a move to Europe and has since shown his quality and confidence at top-club level. He is an amazing shot-stopper, very agile, strong and great at dealing with crosses.

NATIONALITY
Costa Rican

CURRENT CLUB
Paris Saint-Germain

BIRTHDATE	15/12/1986
POSITION	GOALKEEPER
HEIGHT	1.85 M
WEIGHT	80 KG
PREFERRED FOOT	RIGHT

GOALS CONCEDED
241

APPEARANCES
262

PENALTIES SAVED
10

SAVES
796

CLEAN SHEETS
102

PENALTIES FACED
36

CATCHES
144

PUNCHES
108

MAJOR CLUB HONOURS
⚽ Ligue 1: 2020 ⚽ La Liga: 2017 (Real Madrid) ⚽ UEFA Champions League: 2016, 2017, 2018 (Real Madrid)
⚽ UEFA Super Cup: 2014, 2017 (Real Madrid) ⚽ FIFA Club World Cup: 2014, 2016, 2017, 2018 (Real Madrid)

INTERNATIONAL HONOURS
⚽ None to date

ACTIVITY AREAS

NATIONALITY
German

CURRENT CLUB
Bayern Munich

MANUEL NEUER

Manuel Neuer is famous for being football's first sweeper-keeper. He is a fine shot-stopper who commands his penalty area and marshals the defence well. He is also great with the ball at his feet, allowing defenders to play further upfield.

BIRTHDATE	27/03/1986
POSITION	GOALKEEPER
HEIGHT	1.93 M
WEIGHT	92 KG
PREFERRED FOOT	RIGHT

GOALS CONCEDED
470

APPEARANCES
555

PENALTIES SAVED
10

CLEAN SHEETS
246

SAVES
1391

CATCHES
586

PENALTIES FACED
39

PUNCHES
258

MAJOR CLUB HONOURS

⚽ Bundesliga: 2013, 2014, 2015, 2016, 2017, 2018, 2019, 2020 ⚽ UEFA Champions League: 2013, 2020 ⚽ UEFA Super Cup: 2013, 2020 ⚽ FIFA Club World Cup: 2013, 2021

INTERNATIONAL HONOURS

⚽ FIFA World Cup: 2014

ACTIVITY AREAS

DAVID OSPINA

David Ospina is considered to have very few weaknesses. He is excellent with crosses, equally happy punching or catching the ball and a super shot-stopper. Not the tallest of keepers, he makes up for this with his agility and speed off his line.

NATIONAITY
Colombian

CURRENT CLUB
Napoli

BIRTHDATE	31/08/1988
POSITION	GOALKEEPER
HEIGHT	1.83 M
WEIGHT	80 KG
PREFERRED FOOT	RIGHT

GOALS CONCEDED
345

APPEARANCES
302

PENALTIES SAVED
7

CLEAN SHEETS
97

SAVES
890

PENALTIES FACED
38

CATCHES
443

PUNCHES
183

MAJOR CLUB HONOURS
- Coppa Italia: 2020
- FA Cup: 2015, 2017 (Arsenal)

INTERNATIONAL HONOURS
- Copa América: third place 2016

ACTIVITY AREAS

NATIONALITY
English

CURRENT CLUB
Everton

JORDAN PICKFORD

Currently England's No1, Jordan Pickford is an agile and alert keeper who often starts moves from the back. He is also a big-match player and has won matches saving in shoot-outs and scoring in them, too.

BIRTHDATE	07/03/1994
POSITION	GOALKEEPER
HEIGHT	1.85 M
WEIGHT	77 KG
PREFERRED FOOT	LEFT

GOALS CONCEDED
252

APPEARANCES
171

PENALTIES SAVED
4

CLEAN SHEETS
43

SAVES
536

PENALTIES FACED
22

CATCHES
107

PUNCHES
91

MAJOR CLUB HONOURS
⚽ None to date

INTERNATIONAL HONOURS
⚽ UEFA Nations League: third place 2019

ACTIVITY AREAS

100

KASPER SCHMEICHEL

Kasper Schmeichel, the son of the legendary keeper Peter Schmeichel, has many of his father's strengths. He is mentally strong and brilliant in one-on-one situations. He is also superb in the air, commands his penalty area and is a great ball distributor.

NATIONALITY
Danish

CURRENT CLUB
Leicester City

BIRTHDATE	05/11/1986
POSITION	GOALKEEPER
HEIGHT	1.89 M
WEIGHT	89 KG
PREFERRED FOOT	RIGHT

GOALS CONCEDED
309

APPEARANCES
254

PENALTIES SAVED
7

CLEAN SHEETS
82

SAVES
711

PENALTIES FACED
34

CATCHES
183

PUNCHES
112

MAJOR CLUB HONOURS
⚽ Premier League: 2016

INTERNATIONAL HONOURS
⚽ None to date

ACTIVITY AREAS

101

NATIONALITY
Polish

CURRENT CLUB
Juventus

WOJCIECH SZCZĘSNY

Wojciech Szczęsny has grown into one of Europe's top-class keepers. A natural shot-stopper with lightning reflexes, he is also great at controlling his penalty area, dealing with crosses and setting up counter-attacks with quick clearances.

BIRTHDATE	18/04/1990
POSITION	GOALKEEPER
HEIGHT	1.95 M
WEIGHT	90 KG
PREFERRED FOOT	RIGHT

GOALS CONCEDED
378

APPEARANCES
358

PENALTIES SAVED
11

CLEAN SHEETS
126

SAVES
970

PENALTIES FACED
58

CATCHES
324

PUNCHES
149

MAJOR CLUB HONOURS
- ⚽ Serie A: 2018, 2019, 2020
- ⚽ FA Cup: 2014, 2015 (Arsenal)
- ⚽ Coppa Italia: 2018

INTERNATIONAL HONOURS
- ⚽ None to date

ACTIVITY AREAS

MARC-ANDRÉ TER STEGEN

A brilliant sweeper-keeper, Marc-André ter Stegen is simply world class. In addition to his fine goalkeeping qualities, he is exceptional at anticipating opponents who have beaten the offside trap, and can rush off his line to meet the danger.

NATIONALITY
German

CURRENT CLUB
Barcelona

BIRTHDATE	30/04/1992
POSITION	GOALKEEPER
HEIGHT	1.87 M
WEIGHT	85 KG
PREFERRED FOOT	RIGHT

GOALS CONCEDED
350

APPEARANCES
354

PENALTIES SAVED
6

CLEAN SHEETS
140

SAVES
1035

PENALTIES FACED
36

CATCHES
416

PUNCHES
161

MAJOR CLUB HONOURS
⚽ La Liga: 2015, 2016, 2018, 2019 ⚽ UEFA Champions League: 2015 ⚽ UEFA Super Cup: 2015 ⚽ FIFA Club World Cup: 2015 ⚽ Coppa del Rey: 2015, 2016, 2017, 2018

INTERNATIONAL HONOURS
⚽ FIFA Confederations Cup: 2017

ACTIVITY AREAS

MANAGERS

Head coaches are as different to each other as players who play in different positions. But the majority of the 12 featured in this section have one thing in common: they are all winners, either in their domestic leagues or in continental competitions. Some, such as Diego Simeone (pictured), were legendary players in their own right and title winners well before they entered management, while others, such as Liverpool boss Jürgen Klopp, did little on the field but have had great success as the brains behind a top side.

WHAT DO THE STATS MEAN?

GAMES MANAGED
This is the number of matches the coach has been in charge of across their career in top-flight football.

TEAMS MANAGED
The number of clubs, including national sides, that the coach has managed during their career to date.

WINS
This is the number of games the coach has won, including one leg of a cup-tie, even if the tie was lost on aggregate or penalties.

TROPHIES
The trophy list features the domestic honours a coach has won across all the teams they have managed as well as any major European titles.

Did you know?

Retired manager Fabio Capello has won a major league championship in seven (or nine, counting the two revoked titles with Juventus) of his 16 seasons as a coach in Europe's top domestic leagues.

CARLO ANCELOTTI

Formerly an international player, Carlo Ancelotti uses different systems depending on the opposition and players available. His favourite formation is 4—4—2, sometimes in a diamond, other times with four midfielders in a line across the pitch.

NATIONALITY
Italian

CURRENT CLUB
Everton

DEBUT YEAR:	1995
FIRST CLUB:	REGGIANA

CLUBS MANAGED	GAMES	LEAGUE TITLES
10	904	4

WINS	DRAW	LOSSES
515	216	173

CHAMPIONS LEAGUE TROPHIES	EUROPA LEAGUE TROPHIES	OTHER TROPHIES*
3	0	4

MAJOR CLUB HONOURS
- ⚽ UEFA Champions League: 2003, 2007 (Milan), 2014 (Real Madrid)
- ⚽ FIFA Club World Cup: 2003, 2007 (Milan), 2014 (Real Madrid)
- ⚽ UEFA Super Cup: 2007, 2014 (Real Madrid)
- ⚽ UEFA Intertoto Cup: 1999 (Juventus)
- ⚽ Serie A: 2004 (Milan)
- ⚽ Premier League: 2010 (Chelsea)
- ⚽ Ligue 1: 2013 (Paris St Germain)
- ⚽ Copa del Rey: 2014 (Real Madrid)
- ⚽ Bundesliga: 2017 (Bayern Munich)

*Excludes Super Cups

ANTONIO CONTE

Although Antonio Conte varies his tactics and formations, they are always based on a strong defence, so his teams tend to be great counter-attackers. Always animated on the touchline, he instils a great team spirit into his side.

NATIONALITY
Italian

CURRENT CLUB
Inter Milan

DEBUT YEAR:	2006
FIRST CLUB:	AREZZO

CLUBS MANAGED	GAMES	LEAGUE TITLES
8	321	4

WINS	DRAW	LOSSES
206	68	47

CHAMPIONS LEAGUE TROPHIES	EUROPA LEAGUE TROPHIES	OTHER TROPHIES*
0	0	2

MAJOR CLUB HONOURS
- ⚽ Serie A: 2012, 2013, 2014 (Juventus)
- ⚽ Premier League: 2017 (Chelsea)
- ⚽ FA Cup: 2018 (Chelsea)
- ⚽ UEFA Europa League: runner-up 2020

*Excludes Super Cups

HANS-DIETER FLICK

Former Bayern Munich player and assistant manager, Hans-Dieter Flick learned about tactics and player relations working with Italian legend Giovanni Trapattoni, but adopts a more attacking style. He won four trophies in his first season as coach.

NATIONALITY
German

CURRENT CLUB
Bayern Munich
(until May '21)

DEBUT YEAR:	1996
FIRST CLUB:	VICTORIA BAMMENTAL

CLUBS MANAGED	GAMES	LEAGUE TITLES
4	69	1

WINS	DRAW	LOSSES
56	7	6

CHAMPIONS LEAGUE TROPHIES	EUROPA LEAGUE TROPHIES	OTHER TROPHIES*
1	0	3

*Excludes Super Cups

MAJOR CLUB HONOURS
- ⚽ UEFA Champions League: 2020
- ⚽ UEFA Super Cup: 2020
- ⚽ FIFA Club World Cup: 2020
- ⚽ Bundesliga: 2020
- ⚽ DfB Pokal: 2020

PEP GUARDIOLA

Once a great midfielder himself, Pep Guardiola devised the *tika-taka* passing system at Barcelona (2008-12). Disciplined in possession, without the ball his teams press the opposition into making mistakes and then launch rapid counter-attacks.

NATIONALITY
Spanish

CURRENT CLUB
Manchester City

DEBUT YEAR:	2008
FIRST CLUB:	BARCELONA

CLUBS MANAGED	GAMES	LEAGUE TITLES
3	570	8

WINS	DRAW	LOSSES
417	86	67

CHAMPIONS LEAGUE TROPHIES	EUROPA LEAGUE TROPHIES	OTHER TROPHIES*
2	0	12

*Excludes Super Cups

MAJOR CLUB HONOURS
- ⚽ UEFA Champions League: 2009, 2011 (Barcelona)
- ⚽ UEFA Super Cup: 2009, 2011 (Barcelona), 2013 (Bayern Munich)
- ⚽ FIFA Club World Cup: 2009, 2011 (Barcelona), 2013 (Bayern Munich)
- ⚽ La Liga: 2009, 2010, 2011 (Barcelona)
- ⚽ Bundesliga: 2014, 2015, 2016 (Bayern Munich)
- ⚽ Premier League: 2018, 2019
- ⚽ FA Cup: 2019

JÜRGEN KLOPP

NATIONALITY
German

CURRENT CLUB
Liverpool

Jürgen Klopp brings great enthusiasm to the technical area and expects his team to show a similar spirit. His team are strong defensively, try to win back the ball immediately after they lose it and counter-attack at great speed.

DEBUT YEAR: 2001

FIRST CLUB: MAINZ 05

CLUBS MANAGED	GAMES	LEAGUE TITLES
3	656	3

WINS	DRAW	LOSSES
347	154	155

CHAMPIONS LEAGUE TROPHIES	EUROPA LEAGUE TROPHIES	OTHER TROPHIES*
1	0	2

MAJOR CLUB HONOURS
- ⚽ UEFA Champions League: runner-up 2013 (Borussia Dortmund), runner-up 2018, winner 2019
- ⚽ UEFA Super Cup: 2019
- ⚽ FIFA Club World Cup: 2019
- ⚽ Bundesliga: 2011, 2012 (Borussia Dortmund)
- ⚽ DFB-Pokal: 2012 (Borussia Dortmund)
- ⚽ Premier League: 2020

*Excludes Super Cups

JULEN LOPETEGUI

NATIONALITY
Spanish

CURRENT CLUB
Sevilla

Julen Lopetegui likes his teams to be creative in attack and wants his full-backs to give width, dragging defenders out of position and then filling the gaps they leave behind. He preaches a never give up attitude from his teams.

DEBUT YEAR: 2003

FIRST CLUB: RAYO VALLECANO

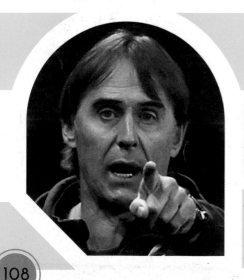

CLUBS MANAGED	GAMES	LEAGUE TITLES
4	116	0

WINS	DRAW	LOSSES
65	27	24

CHAMPIONS LEAGUE TROPHIES	EUROPA LEAGUE TROPHIES	OTHER TROPHIES*
0	1	0

MAJOR CLUB HONOURS
- ⚽ UEFA Europa League: 2020
- ⚽ UEFA Super Cup: runner-up 2020
- ⚽ UEFA Super Cup: runner-up 2018 (Real Madrid)

*Excludes Super Cups

JOSÉ MOURINHO

José Mourinho focuses his team strength on midfield, normally with a player in front of the defence and two or three further upfield. He expects his defenders to be tactically and technically excellent, and tends to pick experienced players.

NATIONALITY
Portuguese

CURRENT CLUB
Roma

DEBUT YEAR: 2000

FIRST CLUB: BENFICA

CLUBS MANAGED	GAMES	LEAGUE TITLES
9	741	8

WINS	DRAW	LOSSES
459	160	123

CHAMPIONS LEAGUE TROPHIES	EUROPA LEAGUE TROPHIES	OTHER TROPHIES*
2	2	8

MAJOR CLUB HONOURS
- UEFA Champions League: 2004 (Porto), 2010 (Inter Milan)
- UEFA Europa League: 2017 (Manchester United)
- UEFA Cup: 2003 (Porto)
- Premier League: 2005, 2006, 2015 (Chelsea)
- FA Cup: 2006 (Chelsea)
- Serie A: 2009, 2010 (Inter Milan)
- Coppa Italia: 2010 (Inter Milan)
- La Liga: 2012 (Real Madrid)
- Copa del Rey: 2011 (Real Madrid)

*Excludes Super Cups

JULIAN NAGELSMANN

Julian Nagelsmann retired from playing aged 24 and moved into coaching while studying sports science at university. He is great at match preparation and is happy to get his teams to change formation with or without possession of the ball.

 NATIONALITY
German

CURRENT CLUB
Bayern Munich

DEBUT YEAR: 2016

FIRST CLUB: 1899 HOFFENHEIM

CLUBS MANAGED	GAMES	LEAGUE TITLES
3	208	0

WINS	DRAW	LOSSES
98	63	47

CHAMPIONS LEAGUE TROPHIES	EUROPA LEAGUE TROPHIES	OTHER TROPHIES*
0	0	0

MAJOR CLUB HONOURS
- None to date

*Excludes Super Cups

MAURICIO POCHETTINO

NATIONALITY
Argentinian

CURRENT CLUB
Paris Saint-Germain

Mauricio Pochettino made his reputation at Barcelona's second club Espanyol before coming to England. He teams play open football, featuring technically good defenders, a spearhead striker and midfielders attacking from deeper positions.

DEBUT YEAR:	2009
FIRST CLUB:	ESPANYOL

CLUBS MANAGED	GAMES	LEAGUE TITLES
4	471	0

WINS	DRAW	LOSSES
216	108	147

CHAMPIONS LEAGUE TROPHIES	EUROPA LEAGUE TROPHIES	OTHER TROPHIES*
0	0	0

MAJOR CLUB HONOURS
- ⚽ UEFA Champions League runner-up 2019 (Tottenham Hotspur)

*Excludes Super Cups

CLAUDIO RANIERI

NATIONALITY
Italian

CURRENT CLUB
Sampdoria

Claudio Ranieri relies on the 4—4—2 formation, with an emphasis on his team's defensive solidity, work-rate, fitness, pressing the opposition and then launching rapid counter-attacks. He is a great motivator and demands strong team spirit.

DEBUT YEAR:	1986
FIRST CLUB:	VIGOR LAMEZIA

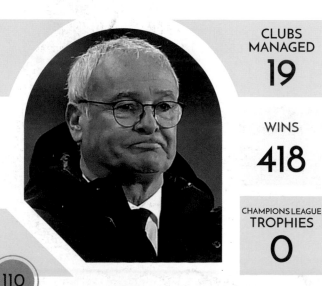

CLUBS MANAGED	GAMES	LEAGUE TITLES
19	934	1

WINS	DRAW	LOSSES
418	254	262

CHAMPIONS LEAGUE TROPHIES	EUROPA LEAGUE TROPHIES	OTHER TROPHIES*
0	0	7

MAJOR CLUB HONOURS
- ⚽ UEFA Super Cup: 2004 (Valencia)
- ⚽ UEFA Intertoto Cup: 1998 (Valencia)
- ⚽ Coppa Italia: 1996 (Fiorentina)
- ⚽ Copa del Rey: 1999 (Valencia)
- ⚽ Premier League: 2016 (Leicester City)

*Excludes Super Cups

DIEGO SIMEONE

Diego Simeone likes to use a formation which is almost a 4–2–2–2 unit, with wide midfielders playing between the two central ones and the strikers. Strong defensively, his teams are great defending set-pieces and dangerous in attack.

NATIONALITY
Argentinian

CURRENT CLUB
Atlético Madrid

DEBUT YEAR: 2006

FIRST CLUB: RACING CLUB

CLUBS MANAGED	GAMES	LEAGUE TITLES
7	479	3

WINS	DRAW	LOSSES
287	109	83

CHAMPIONS LEAGUE TROPHIES	EUROPA LEAGUE TROPHIES	OTHER TROPHIES*
0	2	1

*Excludes Super Cups

MAJOR CLUB HONOURS
- UEFA Champions League: runner-up 2014, 2016
- UEFA Europa League: 2012, 2018
- UEFA Super Cup: 2012, 2018
- La Liga: 2014
- Copa del Rey: 2013

THOMAS TUCHEL

Thomas Tuchel has won multiple trophies. He is flexible, changing tactics to suit the players he has available, and a strong believer in *Gegenpressing*, immediately trying to regain possession rather than dropping into a more defensive mode.

NATIONALITY
German

CURRENT CLUB
Chelsea

DEBUT YEAR: 2007

FIRST CLUB: AUGSBURG II

CLUBS MANAGED	GAMES	LEAGUE TITLES
5	382	2

WINS	DRAW	LOSSES
207	79	96

CHAMPIONS LEAGUE TROPHIES	EUROPA LEAGUE TROPHIES	OTHER TROPHIES*
0	0	2

*Excludes Super Cups

MAJOR CLUB HONOURS
- UEFA Champions League: runner-up 2020 (Paris Saint-Germain)
- Ligue 1: 2019, 2020 (Paris Saint-Germain)
- Coupe de France: 2020 (Paris Saint-Germain)
- DfB Pokal: 2017 (Borussia Dortmund)

NOTES